Criminal Law
sixth edition

GU00976458

Routledge·Cavendish
Taylor & Francis Group
LONDON AND NEW YORK

Sixth edition published 2009
by Routledge-Cavendish
2 Park Square, Milton Park, Abingdon, Oxon OX14 4RN

Simultaneously published in the USA and Canada
by Routledge-Cavendish
270 Madison Ave, New York, NY 10016

Routledge-Cavendish is an imprint of the Taylor & Francis Group, an informa business

© 2006, 2009 Routledge-Cavendish

Previous editions published by Cavendish Publishing Limited
First edition   1997
Second edition   1999
Third edition   2002
Fourth edition   2004

Typeset in Rotis by RefineCatch Limited, Bungay, Suffolk
Printed and bound in Great Britain by Ashford Colour Press Ltd, Gosport, Hants

British Library Cataloguing in Publication Data
A catalogue record for this book is available from the British Library

Library of Congress Cataloging in Publication Data
Criminal law.—6th ed.
     p. cm.
1. Criminal law—England.   2. Criminal law—Wales.
     KD7869.C73 2008
     345.42—dc22

                                      2008018364

ISBN10: 0-415-45687-8 (pbk)
ISBN13: 978-0-415-45687-6 (pbk)

Contents

Table of Cases

Table of Statutes

How to use this book

Welcome to this new edition of Routledge-Cavendish Criminal Law Lawcards. In response to student feedback, we've added some new features to these new editions to give you all the support and preparation you need in order to face your law exams with confidence.

Inside this book you will find:

■ NEW tables of cases and statutes for ease of reference

■ Revision Checklist

We've summarised the key topics you will need to know for your law exams and broken them down into a handy revision checklist. Check them out at the beginning of each chapter, then after you have the chapter down, revisit the checklist and tick each topic off as you gain knowledge and confidence.

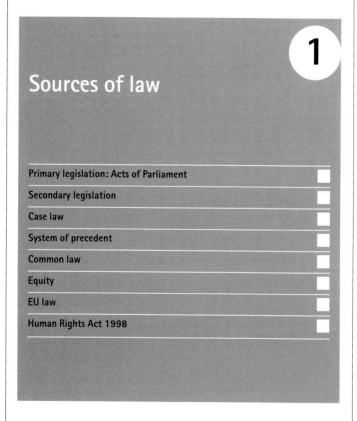

1

Sources of law

Primary legislation: Acts of Parliament	☐
Secondary legislation	☐
Case law	☐
System of precedent	☐
Common law	☐
Equity	☐
EU law	☐
Human Rights Act 1998	☐

■ Key Cases

We've identified the key cases that are most likely to come up in exams. To help you to ensure that you can cite cases with ease, we've included a brief account of the case and judgment for a quick aide-memoire.

HENDY LENNOX v GRAHAME PUTTICK [1984]

Basic facts

Diesel engines were supplied, subject to a *Romalpa* clause, then fitted to generators. Each engine had a serial number. When the buyer became insolvent the seller sought to recover one engine. The Receiver argued that the process of fitting the engine to the generator passed property to the buyer. The court disagreed and allowed the seller to recover the still identifiable engine despite the fact that some hours of work would be required to disconnect it.

Relevance

If the property remains identifiable and is not irredeemably changed by the manufacturing process a *Romalpa* clause may be viable.

■ Companion Website

At the end of each chapter you will be prompted to visit the Routledge-Cavendish Lawcards companion website where you can test your understanding online with specially prepared multiple-choice questions, as well as revise the key terms with our online glossary.

You should now be confident that you would be able to tick all of the boxes on the checklist at the beginning of this chapter. To check your knowledge of Sources of law why not visit the companion website and take the Multiple Choice Question test. Check your understanding of the terms and vocabulary used in this chapter with the flashcard glossary.

■ Exam Practice

Once you've acquired the basic knowledge, you'll want to put it to the test. The Routledge-Cavendish Questions and Answers provides examples of the kinds of questions that you will face in your exams, together with suggested answer plans and a fully-worked model answer. We've included one example free at the end of this book to help you put your technique and understanding into practice.

QUESTION 1

What are the main sources of law today?

Answer plan

This is, apparently, a very straightforward question, but the temptation is to ignore the European Community (EU) as a source of law and to over-emphasise custom as a source. The following structure does not make these mistakes:

■ in the contemporary situation, it would not be improper to start with the EU as a source of UK law;

■ then attention should be moved on to domestic sources of law: statute and common law;

■ the increased use of delegated legislation should be emphasised;

■ custom should be referred to, but its extremely limited operation must be emphasised.

ANSWER

European law

Since the UK joined the European Economic Community (EEC), now the EU, it has progressively but effectively passed the power to create laws which are operative in this country to the wider European institutions. The UK is now subject to Community law, not just as a direct consequence of the various treaties of accession passed by the UK Parliament, but increasingly, it is subject to the secondary legislation generated by the various institutions of the EU.

1

The nature of a crime

A crime is conduct which has been defined as such by statute or by common law. To be convicted of a crime, two essential elements must be proved:

1   The *Actus Reus* – the prohibited act, omission, or state of affairs; and
2   The *Mens Rea* – the required state of mind, such as intent or recklessness

The main exception to this is crimes of strict liability where no *mens rea* need be proved.

 = *actus reus* + *mens rea* + absence of a valid defence

The prosecution must prove the existence of the *actus reus* and *mens rea* beyond reasonable doubt. This is sometimes referred to as the *Woolmington* rule (*Woolmington v DPP* [1935]).

GENERAL PRINCIPLES OF CRIMINAL LAW

See diagram on facing page.

CHARACTERISTICS OF AN *ACTUS REUS*

Definition
An *actus reus* consists of all the elements in the statutory or common law definition of the offence except the defendant's mental element.

General principles of criminal law

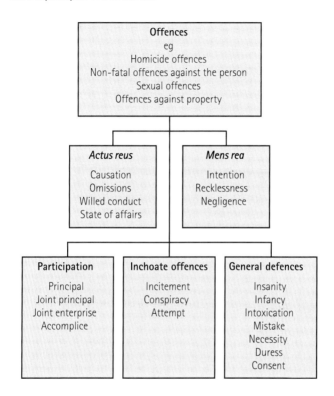

Analysis of the *actus reus*

An *actus reus* can be identified by looking at the definition of the offence in question and subtracting the *mens rea* requirements of 'knowingly', 'intentionally', 'recklessly', 'maliciously', 'dishonestly' or 'negligently'.

The *actus reus* states the conduct or omission required for the offence, the specified surrounding circumstances in which it must take place and any consequences if required by the offence.

This process of identifying and analysing an *actus reus* can be illustrated in relation to s 1(1) of the Criminal Damage Act 1971, which provides:

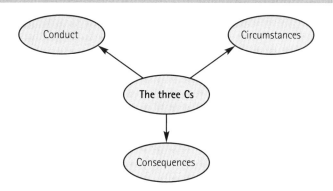

A person who without lawful excuse destroys or damages any property belonging to another intending to destroy or damage any such property or being reckless as to whether such property would be destroyed or damaged shall be guilty of an offence.

Once expressions relating to the *mens rea* requirements of intention or recklessness have been subtracted, the *actus reus* consists of destroying or damaging property belonging to another.

> Conduct = the act of destroying or damaging
>
> Circumstances = the fact that the property must belong to another
>
> Consequences = the resultant damage or destruction

CONDUCT AND RESULT CRIMES

In analysing the *actus reus* we can separate 'conduct only' crimes from 'result' crimes. An example of a conduct crime is blackmail. The offence is committed where the defendant makes an unwarranted demand with menaces, with a view to gain or with a view to causing loss to another (s 21 of the Theft Act 1968). The making of such a demand is sufficient to establish the *actus reus*; it matters not whether the desired consequence of gain to the defendant (or loss to the victim) actually occurs. Therefore, the offence can be committed even if the demand never reaches the intended victim (*Treacy v DPP* [1971]).

By contrast, a result crime requires the prosecution to prove, in order to establish the *actus reus*, that the defendant caused a particular consequence specified by the offence. For example, under s 15 of the Theft Act 1968, obtaining property by deception, it must be proved that someone has been deceived by the defendant's deception and that property was obtained by him as a result of that deception. In this example it has to be proven that the defendant's conduct caused two results: someone was deceived and property was obtained.

SPECIFIC ISSUES IN ESTABLISHING THE *ACTUS REUS*

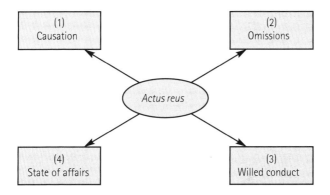

(1) CAUSATION

Issues of causation most frequently arise in relation to homicide cases, but they can arise in respect of any 'result' crime. We have noted that result crimes require the prosecution to prove that the defendant *caused* the result or consequence specified by the offence. Issues of causation cannot arise with 'conduct' crimes, as they are not concerned with results and consequences.

Establishing causation is a two-stage process:

1   establishing factual causation;
2   establishing legal causation.

Causation is most helpfully illustrated through homicide cases. To establish the *actus reus* of homicide it is necessary to prove that the defendant caused the victim's death.

Causation in fact

The first step in establishing causation is to ask 'was the defendant's act a *cause in fact* of the specified consequence (for example, death in the case of homicide)?'. This question can be answered by asking: 'But for what the defendant did would the consequence have occurred?' If the answer is no, causation *in fact* is established.

An example of where the prosecution failed to establish causation in fact is the case of *R v White* [1910]. The defendant had put cyanide into his mother's drink, but the medical evidence showed that she died of heart failure before the poison could take effect. Consequently, the answer to the question 'But for what the defendant did would she have died?' is 'yes'. She would have died anyway.

Causation in law

Just because the prosecution establish that the defendant's act was a cause in fact of the prohibited consequence, does not necessarily mean that the defendant is liable. The prosecution must establish a legal chain of causation between the defendant's acts and the specified consequence. This can become difficult where other individuals or events also contribute to the prohibited harm.

One approach to establishing causation in law is to consider whether the defendant's act was an 'operative and substantial' cause of the consequence in question. Only if the defendant's act could be said to have merely provided the setting in which some other cause operated would the chain of causation be broken (*R v Smith* [1959]).

It should be noted that 'substantial', in this context, simply means anything more than a *de minimis* (trivial) contribution. For example, in *R v Hennigan* [1971] it was held that the defendant could be found guilty of causing death by dangerous driving even though he was only 20 per cent to blame for the accident.

It should also be noted that an 'operative and substantial' cause need not be the direct cause of the specified consequence. This can arise where a victim reacts to threats made by the defendant. For example, in *R v Roberts* [1971], the direct cause of injury was the act of the victim herself (she had jumped from a moving car after the defendant had sexually assaulted her).

Nonetheless the defendant was convicted of an assault causing actual bodily harm.

An alternative approach to the 'operative and substantial' test for establishing causation in law is to consider whether the result specified in the *actus reus* was a reasonably foreseeable consequence of what the defendant had done. Thus, in *R v Pagett* [1983], the defendant was held to have caused the death of a girl hostage he was holding in front of him when he fired at armed police officers who returned fire, killing the girl. It was reasonably foreseeable in the circumstances that the officers would instinctively return fire and hit the victim.

▶ R v PAGETT [1983]

The legal chain of causation is not broken where a third party's actions are a reasonably foreseeable response to the defendant's actions.

Facts
The defendant used his girlfriend as a human shield and fired at police. The police officers fired back and killed the girl.

Held
The defendant had caused death as it was reasonably foreseeable that the police officers would return fire on the defendant.

The 'thin skull' rule
As in tort, the defendant must take his victim as he finds him. For example, if the victim of an assault is unusually vulnerable to physical injury as a result of a medical condition or old age, the defendant must accept liability for any unusually serious consequences which result. In *R v Blaue* [1975] it was stated that the defendant had to take 'the whole man, not just the physical man'. The defendant was held to have caused the death of a Jehovah's Witness whom he had stabbed, notwithstanding that she had refused a blood transfusion that would have probably saved her life. He had to take his victim as he found her, including not just her physical condition, but also her religious beliefs.

Novus actus interveniens

A defendant will not legally have caused the specified consequence if there was a *novus actus interveniens* (or new intervening act) sufficient to break the legal chain of causation. This may be an act of the victim, an act of a third party, or an unforeseeable natural event. The effect of the intervening act must be so overwhelming that the defendant's assault is relegated to the status of mere historical background.

Self-neglect

Although it may not be reasonably foreseeable that the victim will neglect his wounds, it seems that such neglect will not break the chain of causation (*R v Smith* [1959]). Even if the victim aggravates the condition caused by the defendant, the chain of causation will not be broken. In *R v Dear* [1996] the defendant had repeatedly slashed the victim with a knife after being told that he had sexually interfered with the defendant's 12-year-old daughter. The victim died two days later. The defendant argued that the victim caused his own death by re-opening his wounds and refusing to allow an ambulance to be called, so that he bled to death. There was also evidence of a suicide note left by the victim. The defendant's conviction was nevertheless upheld on the basis that the defendant's conduct was still an operating and significant cause of death.

Death caused by medical treatment

Where death is caused by the medical treatment of a wound, the original attacker is held liable for homicide. This is so even in the case of *negligent* medical treatment (*R v Smith* [1959]).

However, it seems that in rare cases 'palpably wrong' medical treatment will break the chain of causation (*R v Jordan* [1956]). In *R v Cheshire* [1991], it was stated that, unless the negligent treatment was 'so independent of the accused's acts' and 'so potent in causing death' that the contribution made by his acts was insignificant, the chain of causation would not be broken (and see *R v Mellor* [1996]).

There is some authority for the suggestion that the administration of pain-saving drugs which incidentally shorten life by a very short period (hours or days, but not weeks or months) would not amount to a cause in law of death (*R v Adams* [1957]).

Causation

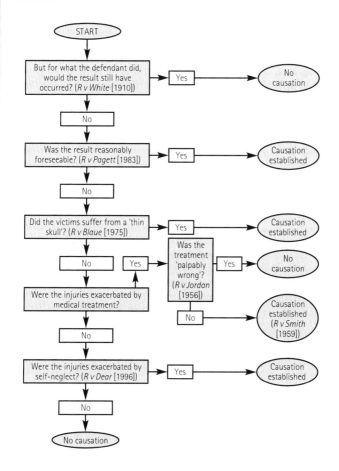

(2) OMISSIONS

As a general rule, a person is not criminally liable for what they do not do. However, there are exceptions where the defendant is under a positive duty to act. In these exceptional situations, the defendant will have caused the *actus reus* by doing nothing.

❭ R v JORDAN [1956]

Medical treatment will only break the legal chain of causation where the treatment is palpably wrong.

Facts

The victim was stabbed by the defendant and the wound was nearly healed. The victim was then given the wrong medication in hospital from which he died.

Held

The wound was not the operative and substantial cause of death and the medical treatment broke the legal chain of causation. The defendant's conviction for murder was quashed.

Liability for omissions can occur where there is a duty of care to children or where there is an assumption of care for another. For example, a parent who deliberately neglects a child such that they starve to death may be guilty of murder (*R v Gibbens and Proctor* [1918]). In *R v Stone and Dobinson* [1977] Stone's ill sister came to live with him and his mistress, Dobinson. The sister was initially able to look after herself but her condition deteriorated, and she became bed-ridden. The correct medical help was not sought and she eventually died from extreme neglect. Both defendants were convicted of manslaughter.

Liability may arise where there is a failure to discharge official or contractual obligations. In *R v Pittwood* [1902] a level-crossing operator omitted to close the crossing gates at the appropriate time, causing death to a user. Pittwood was convicted of gross negligence manslaughter. Several statutory provisions also impose criminal sanctions for failure or omission to act. For example, road traffic law makes it an offence to fail to stop after an accident. (Also refer to *R v Dytham* [1979].)

Liability can also arise where there is a failure to avert a danger of one's own making. In *R v Miller* [1983] the defendant was 'sleeping rough' in a building and fell asleep whilst smoking a cigarette. He awoke to find his mattress smouldering but did nothing about the danger – he simply moved to another room and went back to sleep. The fire subsequently spread. He was convicted of arson for his failure to act.

Omissions

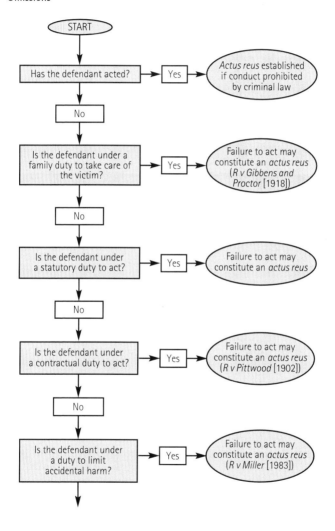

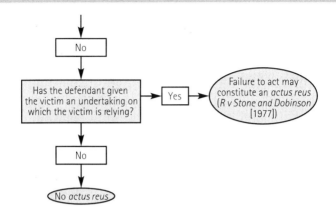

(3) THE CONDUCT MUST BE WILLED

Where, as is usually the case, the *actus reus* of an offence specifies some form of conduct, it must be proved that the defendant consciously willed the relevant action.

If the defendant's muscles acted without the control of his mind he is not blameworthy and will be able to plead automatism (*Bratty v AG for Northern Ireland* [1963]). If successful the defendant is acquitted.

Evidence of an 'external factor' is crucial to establish a plea of automatism (*R v Quick* [1973]; *R v Sullivan* [1984]). External factors causing transitory malfunctioning of the mind might include violence, drugs (including anaesthetics), alcohol or hypnotic influences. Where the cause of the behaviour is 'internal', such as a 'disease of the mind' or a disease of the body, the relevant defence will be that of insanity rather than automatism (*R v Hennessy* [1989]).

Impaired, reduced or partial control by the defendant will not found a defence of automatism. A total loss of voluntary control is required (*AG's Reference (No 2 of 1992)* [1993]).

If the defendant is at fault in bringing about the autonomic state, for example, by voluntarily taking dangerous drugs, he will have a defence to crimes of 'specific intent', but not to those of 'basic intent' (*R v Lipman* [1970];

R v Bailey [1983]). For an explanation of crimes of 'specific intent', see intoxication in Chapter 6.

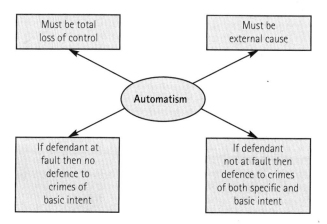

(4) STATE OF AFFAIRS OFFENCES

A crime may be defined so as not to require any willed action at all; it may be enough if a specified 'state of affairs' is proved to exist. For example, s 4 of the Road Traffic Act 1988 provides that a person who, when in charge of a motor vehicle on a road or other public place, is unfit to drive through drink or drugs, commits an offence. It is not the action of taking charge of the vehicle or that of *becoming* unfit which constitutes the offence, but simply the state of *being unfit.*

Thus, the defendant in *R v Larsonneur* [1933] was convicted of being found in the UK, contrary to the Aliens Order of 1920, despite the fact that she had been forcibly brought into the jurisdiction by the immigration authorities.

Similarly, the defendant in *Winzar v Chief Constable of Kent* [1983] was convicted of being found drunk on the highway, despite the fact that he had been deposited there by police officers.

'State of affairs' offences are often also offences of 'strict liability' (see below). It is not surprising that they tend to be regarded as unjustifiably harsh, since not only is there no need to prove any action by the defendant, but also there is no need to prove any *mens rea* either.

THE NATURE OF *MENS REA*

Definition

The term *mens rea* refers to the mental element in the definition of a crime. This mental element is usually denoted by words such as 'intentionally', 'knowingly', 'recklessly', 'maliciously' or 'negligently'.

INTENTION

The *mens rea* required for some of the most serious crimes such as murder and wounding or causing grievous bodily harm contrary to s 18 of the Offences Against the Person Act 1861 is intention. Intention has an ordinary meaning and a more complex meaning when applied in criminal law. The first form is direct intention which arises when the defendant aims to bring about the consequence. The more complex interpretation of intention is referred to by criminal lawyers as oblique intent, although the courts never adopt this term. This has proven difficult to define and there have been many cases leading towards the current position. In *Nedrick* [1986] Lord Lane CJ stated that,

> the jury should be directed that they are not entitled to infer the necessary intention unless they feel sure that death or serious bodily harm was a virtual certainty (barring some unforeseen intervention) as a result of the defendant's actions and that the defendant appreciated that such was the case.

This seems to be the current position following *Woollin* [1998] and *Matthews* [2003].

As a result it means that a defendant has intended a result even if it was not their direct intention to do so. This will happen where the jury feel sure that the prohibited harm was virtually certain to happen following the defendant's actions and the jury are also sure that the defendant realised his actions were virtually certain to bring about the harm. This means that different juries may indeed draw different conclusions about the same set of facts.

RECKLESSNESS

The current definition of recklessness has been settled by the House of Lords in *R v G* [2004] who took a subjective approach. This approach is often referred to as *Cunningham* recklessness after an earlier decision. This means that a person will only be reckless if they foresee the risk of harm their actions caused. *It is only important what the defendant foresaw* and not what a reasonable person would foresee.

In *R v G* the two defendants aged 12 and 11 lit some newspapers in the back yard of a shop and then threw them under a dustbin. They left the scene before putting the fire out and it spread to the shop causing significant damage to the property. The court took the ages of the defendants into account and found that they did not appreciate the risk that the fire would spread as it did. In making its decision the Court overruled the previous definition of reckless-ness for criminal damage, *Caldwell*. This was a narrow objective concept and considered harsh. Under *Caldwell* a defendant would be found to be reckless if the risk taken would have been obvious to a reasonable prudent person, even if the individual did not appreciate the risk. If *R v G* had applied the *Caldwell* approach the ages of the defendant would not be relevant and they would have been convicted of arson. Only the subjective concept of recklessness remains now that *Caldwell* has been overruled.

*Recklessness: Caldwell overruled
It is now settled that a *subjective* and narrow concept of recklessness as adopted in *R v Cunningham* [1957] has prevailed, as opposed to an *objective* and wider concept, as adopted in *R v Caldwell* [1982]. *Cunningham* imposes liability only on defendants who *consciously* take unjustified risks, whereas *Caldwell* extended liability to defendants who were unaware that they were running an unjustified risk, provided that a jury thought that the risk would have been obvious to a reasonably prudent bystander. Following the abolition of the offence of causing death by reckless driving, the approach adopted in *Caldwell* appeared to be confined to offences of criminal damage. However, *Caldwell* was overruled by the House of Lords in *R v G and Another* [2003] and so the last remaining application of the objective concept of recklessness has apparently been removed. Therefore, all references to recklessness as a requisite *mens rea* should now be understood in the subjective or *Cunningham* sense.

The main forms of *mens rea* are as follows:

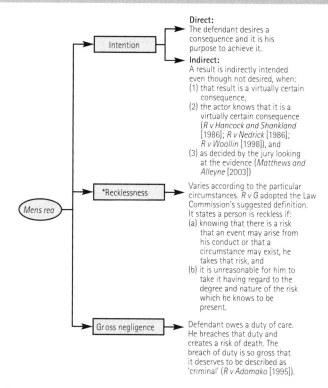

Intention

Direct:
The defendant desires a consequence and it is his purpose to achieve it.

Indirect:
A result is indirectly intended even though not desired, when:
(1) that result is a virtually certain consequence,
(2) the actor knows that it is a virtually certain consequence (*R v Hancock and Shankland* [1986]; *R v Nedrick* [1986]; *R v Woollin* [1998]), and
(3) as decided by the jury looking at the evidence (*Matthews and Alleyne* [2003])

Mens rea

*Recklessness

Varies according to the particular circumstances. *R v G* adopted the Law Commission's suggested definition. It states a person is reckless if:
(a) knowing that there is a risk that an event may arise from his conduct or that a circumstance may exist, he takes that risk, and
(b) it is unreasonable for him to take it having regard to the degree and nature of the risk which he knows to be present.

Gross negligence

Defendant owes a duty of care. He breaches that duty and creates a risk of death. The breach of duty is so gross that it deserves to be described as 'criminal' (*R v Adomako* [1995]).

Blamelessness

A person is blameless if they have acted reasonably in the circumstances. However, even 'blameless' behaviour can attract criminal sanctions in the case of crimes of strict liability.

Transferred malice

If the defendant, with the *mens rea* of a particular crime, does an act which causes the *actus reus* of the same crime, he is guilty, even though the result, in some respects, is an unintended one (*R v Latimer* [1886]).

However, if the defendant, with the *mens rea* of a particular crime, does an act which causes the *actus reus* of another crime, he will not be liable under the doctrine of transferred malice (*R v Pembliton* [1874]).

Transferred malice 1

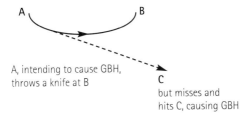

A, intending to cause GBH,
throws a knife at B

C
but misses and
hits C, causing GBH

A is guilty of causing GBH to C under the doctrine of transferred malice since he has caused the *actus reus* of an offence with the requisite *mens rea* for the same offence.

Transferred malice 2

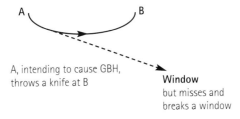

A, intending to cause GBH,
throws a knife at B

Window
but misses and
breaks a window

A is not guilty of criminal damage to the window; the doctrine of transferred malice does not operate since he has caused the *actus reus* of one offence with the *mens rea* of a different offence (however, if the prosecution proved that A was reckless in relation to damaging the window by throwing an object in the vicinity, then he would be liable under normal principles).

In *AG's Reference (No 3 of 1994)* [1997], the House of Lords confirmed the existence of the doctrine of transferred malice, but declined to extend the principle to what it regarded as a 'double transfer' of intent. In this case, the defendant had stabbed a woman whom he knew to be pregnant. She recovered, but there was evidence that the child was born prematurely as a result of the wound to the mother and, as a result of the premature birth, died 120 days later. The House of Lords considered this case to involve a 'double transfer' of intent from the mother to the foetus and from the foetus to the child.

COINCIDENCE OF *ACTUS REUS* AND *MENS REA*

The *mens rea* must coincide at some point in time with the act which causes the *actus reus* (*R v Jakeman* [1983]). However, the courts are sometimes prepared to hold that the *actus reus* consisted of a continuing act and that the defendant is liable if he formed the requisite *mens rea* at some point during this continuing act.

In *R v Thabo Meli* [1954] the defendants attacked a man in accordance with a preconceived plan. Believing him to be dead, they threw his body over a cliff, making his death look like an accident. Medical evidence revealed that the final cause of his death was in fact exposure at the foot of the cliff. The defendants argued that the act of throwing the victim over the cliff was not accompanied by the requisite *mens rea*. They were nonetheless convicted of murder on the basis that the series of acts resulting in death could not be divided up and it was sufficient that the defendants had the requisite *mens rea* in relation to the first attack.

It seems that the continuing act will continue for as long as the defendant is about the business of committing or covering up the crime (*R v Church* [1966], *R v Le Brun* [1992] and see *AG's Reference (No 3 of 1994)* [1997]).

You should now be confident that you would be able to tick all of the boxes on the checklist at the beginning of this chapter. To check your knowledge of The nature of a crime why not visit the companion website and take the Multiple Choice Question test. Check your understanding of the terms and vocabulary used in this chapter with the flashcard glossary.

2

Inchoate offences and participation

Inchoate liability can occur where the defendant progresses some way towards the commission of an offence, but does not necessarily commit the completed offence.

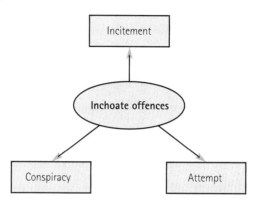

The prosecution have the discretion to charge a defendant with an inchoate offence, even where the completed offence appears to have been committed. This strategy might be adopted where there are likely to be evidential problems with pursuing a prosecution for the full offence.

On the other hand, the prosecution are not at liberty to charge a defendant with *both* an inchoate offence and a completed crime in relation to the same criminal act.

However, where the completed offence is committed, a person who has incited or conspired to commit that offence will become a participant and could incur liability as an accomplice.

INCITEMENT AT COMMON LAW

Definition

An incitement consists of encouraging or pressurising another to commit an offence. The defendant is the incitor. The person he seeks to incite is the incitee.

Unlike conspiracy and attempt, incitement remains primarily a common law offence, but there are also a number of offences of incitement defined by statute. Statutory examples include incitement to murder (s 4 **Offences Against**

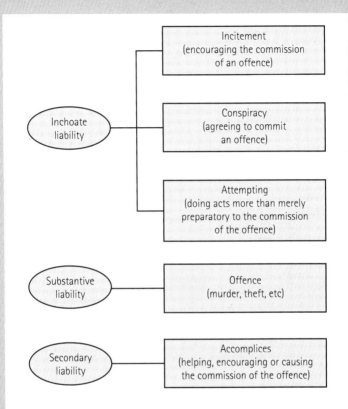

the Person Act 1861) and incitement to commit an offence under the Misuse of Drugs Act 1971 (s 19). The following discussion concerns incitement at common law, but the statutory offences are governed by similar principles.

Actus reus

The central conduct of the offence can take various forms, such as suggesting, proposing, requesting, encouraging, persuading, threatening or pressurising another to commit an offence (*Race Relations Board v Applin* [1973]).

Incitement may also be implied: in *Invicta Plastics Ltd v Clare* [1976] a 'Radatec' device to detect police radar traps was advertised in a motoring magazine, inciting an offence contrary to the Wireless Telegraphy Act 1949.

It is necessary that the incitement is communicated to the incitee (*R v Banks* [1873]), but there is no need for the incitee to act on the incitement (*R v Higgins* [1801]).

The *actus reus* occurs when the defendant *seeks* to persuade. It does not matter whether the 'incitee' actually commits the substantive offence (*DPP v Armstrong* [2000]).

If the incitor tries, but fails, to communicate the incitement, then he would be liable of the offence of attempted incitement (*R v Ransford* [1874]).

Offences that cannot be incited

It is improper to charge incitement in relation to certain other inchoate offences. Incitement to commit statutory or common-law conspiracy was abolished by the **Criminal Law Act 1977** (s 5(7)); but it appears that there is an offence of inciting incitement (*R v Sirat* [1986]), provided this does not amount to the abolished incitement to conspire (*R v Evans* [1986]).

A member of a class of people that a particular offence is designed to protect cannot be liable for inciting that offence (*R v Tyrrell* [1894]). Thus, a girl under the age of 16 could not be guilty of inciting a man to have sexual intercourse with her since she is a victim that the offence of unlawful sexual intercourse is designed to protect.

Mens rea

There are two elements to the *mens rea*. First the defendant must intend to incite and second the defendant must intend that the incitee will act on the incitement (*Invicta Plastics v Clare* [1976]).

The accused must also believe that the person he incites will act with the *mens rea* required for that offence. By contrast, a terrorist who posts a letter bomb does not incite postal workers to commit an offence, but uses them as his innocent agents. The defendant need only believe that the incitee will possess the requisite *mens rea*; the offence is made out even where they do not actually possess the *mens rea*. For example, in *DPP v Armstrong* [2000] a police officer, posing as a provider of pornography, received a request from the defendant to provide photographs of underage girls. The Court of Appeal held that the defendant could be guilty of incitement notwithstanding that the police officer had no intention to commit the offence.

IMPOSSIBILITY

As something of an anomaly, it appears that the offence of incitement remains governed by the common law principle that the defendant cannot be guilty of inciting another to commit a crime that it is impossible to commit. (The common law defence of impossibility has been removed in relation to the statutory offences of Conspiracy and Attempt by the Criminal Attempts Act 1981.) For example, the defendant cannot be convicted of inciting someone to handle goods that are not proved to be stolen, nor of inciting someone to extract cocaine from a substance which contains none (*DPP v Nock* [1978]). However, the courts have taken a narrow view of what is impossible. For example, in *DPP v Armstrong* [2000] the court decided that it was not impossible to incite a police officer provocateur to provide child pornography; if he had wanted to, he could have retrieved such material from police stores. In *R v Fitzmaurice* [1983], the defendant recruited three men to rob a woman he believed would be carrying wages from a bank in Bow (East London). In fact, the defendant had been set up by his father: no such woman existed and the police were lying in wait to arrest the three recruited men. It was argued that the proposed robbery was impossible, but the Court of Appeal disagreed. The offence incited by the defendant was one of 'robbing a woman at Bow' and 'by no stretch of the imagination was that an impossible offence to carry out'. The distinction appears to be that the defence is available where the offence could never be possible (eg killing Queen Victoria) and one where 'a supervening event' makes completion impossible. In *Smith and Turner* [2004] the defendants were found liable for inciting the offence of handling stolen goods when they persuaded X to receive goods that were to be stolen later.

CONSPIRACY

Section 1(1) of the Criminal Law Act 1977 created a statutory offence of conspiracy and abolished, with two exceptions, the old common law offence of conspiracy.

STATUTORY CONSPIRACY

Definition
The statutory offence of conspiracy is created by s 1(1) of the Criminal Law Act 1977, as amended by s 5 of the Criminal Attempts Act 1981, which provides:

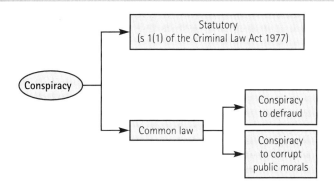

... if a person agrees with any other person or persons that a course of conduct shall be pursued which, if the agreement is carried out in accordance with their intentions, either:

(a) will necessarily amount to or involve the commission of any offence or offences by one or more of the parties to the agreement; or

(b) would do so but for the existence of facts which render the commission of the offence or any of the offences impossible,

he is guilty of conspiracy to commit the offence or offences in question.

Actus reus

The *actus reus* of a statutory conspiracy consists of an agreement between two or more persons to embark on a 'course of conduct' that will necessarily involve the commission of an offence by one of the parties.

It appears that merely talking about the possibility of committing an offence is not sufficient to constitute an agreement (*R v O'Brien* [1974]).

The parties must agree to commit the same crime. In *Taylor* [2002] where the first defendant agreed to import Class A drugs and the second defendant agreed to import Class B drugs no conspiracy had occurred.

Where the parties have agreed to commit the same crime, the conspiracy to commit that crime is complete as soon as the agreement has been made.

Liability remains regardless of whether the agreed offence is committed or if a party changes their mind (*Barnard* [1980]).

The agreement must be communicated between the parties to the conspiracy (*R v Scott* [1979]). However, it is not necessary for every party to a conspiracy to be aware of the existence of every other party. The agreement can take the form of a *chain*, where A agrees with B who then agrees with C and so on, a *wheel*, where numerous parties agree on the same course of conduct with one central figure, or a *cluster*, where several parties simultaneously agree.

Chain

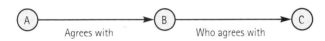

Wheel

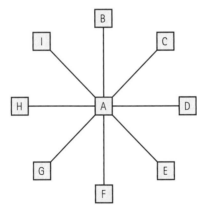

A person cannot be guilty of conspiracy to commit an offence if he is an intended victim of that offence (s 2(1) of the Criminal Law Act 1977).

Section 1(1), para (b) of the Criminal Law Act 1977 makes it clear that, as far as *statutory* conspiracy is concerned, the fact that the agreement is impossible to carry out is no bar to liability (impossibility may still be a defence to a charge of common law conspiracy).

Cluster

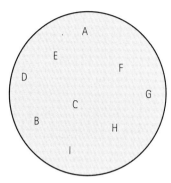

A person shall not be guilty of conspiracy if the only other person with whom he agrees is his spouse (s 2(2)(a)); a child under the age of 10 (s 2(2)(b)); or an intended victim of the agreed offence (s 2(2)(c)).

If the words 'necessarily amount to ... the commission of any offence' were construed strictly, it would be impossible to secure any convictions for conspiracies to commit *possible* offences. For example, suppose that A agrees with B to put a deadly poison into C's food. At first sight, this appears to be a clear case of conspiracy to murder, but it could be argued that this course of conduct would not *necessarily* have amounted to the offence in question; C might not be hungry, or might drop the plate, or might not die. Paradoxically, if the offence was impossible, perhaps because C was already dead at the time of the agreement, then there would be liability for conspiracy to murder since, as we have seen, impossibility is no defence.

In order to avoid this kind of anomalous result, the courts have interpreted 'necessarily' not to mean that the offence must inevitably be committed but that the offence would be necessarily committed *if* the agreement was carried out in accordance with the conspirators' intentions (*R v Jackson* [1985]). According to this interpretation, A and B would be guilty of conspiracy to murder since the intended result of their common plan was the death of C.

Mens rea

There appear to be two elements to the *mens rea* for conspiracy. First, each defendant should have knowledge of any facts or circumstances specified in the substantive offence. Secondly, each defendant should intend the conspiracy to be carried out and the relevant offence committed.

Difficulties have arisen with the second element. In *R v Anderson* [1986] a co-conspirator (the defendant) provided wire cutters to another prisoner to facilitate an escape; the defendant claimed that his only interest was money and that he did not believe the escape would succeed and therefore could not have intended it. In upholding a conviction for conspiracy, Lord Bridge decided, firstly, that a defendant can be convicted of conspiracy without having the intention that the agreement be carried out, and secondly, it is sufficient *mens rea* if, and only if, the defendant intended to play some part in the agreed course of conduct in furtherance of the criminal purpose. Both propositions are now widely considered to be wrong but they have not been expressly overruled. The first proposition is difficult to reconcile with s 1(1) of the Criminal Law Act 1977 which requires there to be an agreement which if carried out *in accordance with their intentions* would necessarily amount to the commission of an offence. The Privy Council subsequently held in *Yip Chiu-Cheung v R* [1994] that it must be established that each conspirator intended the agreement to be carried out, but *Anderson* remains the highest authority. Lord Bridge's second proposition has also been criticised, as it would appear to exclude from the criminal sanction those who plan but do not take part in offences ('godfathers'). This proposition was 'radically' re-interpreted by the Court of Appeal in *R v Siracusa* [1989], such that agreeing 'to play some part' would include doing nothing to stop the unlawful activity.

Note that it was accepted in *R v Siracusa* that the *mens rea* sufficient to support the substantive offence will not necessarily suffice for conspiracy to commit that offence. For example, while the lesser intention to do grievous bodily harm is sufficient *mens rea* to commit murder, the *full* intention to kill is required to support a charge of conspiracy to murder. See below in relation to the *mens rea* for an attempt.

COMMON LAW CONSPIRACY

Section 5(2) and (3) of the Criminal Law Act 1977 preserves two forms of common law conspiracy: conspiracy to defraud and conspiracy to corrupt public morals or outrage public decency.

Common law or statutory conspiracy?

According to s 12 of the Criminal Justice Act 1987, statutory conspiracy and common law conspiracy are not mutually exclusive. The prosecution can choose which offence to charge in cases of overlap.

Impossibility

Impossibility is no defence to a charge of statutory conspiracy (s 1(1)(b) of the Criminal Law Act 1977), but may be a defence to a common law conspiracy. See 'Incitement' above.

ATTEMPT

Definition

By s 1(1) of the Criminal Attempts Act 1981:

> If with intent to commit an offence to which this section applies, a person does an act which is more than merely preparatory to the commission of the offence, he is guilty of attempting to commit the offence.

The judge decides whether there is sufficient evidence to put to the jury, but it is the jury who must decide whether the defendant's acts have gone beyond mere preparation and thus come within the s 1(1) definition of an attempt (*R v Griffin* [1993] and see s 4(3) of the Criminal Attempts Act 1981).

Actus reus

It must be proved that the defendant has gone beyond mere preparation, although it is no longer necessary for the 'last act' prior to the commission of the offence to have been committed (*R v Gullefer* [1987]).

Lord Lane in *Gullefer* said that the 1981 Act sought to steer a 'midway course' between mere preparation, on the one hand, and the 'last act' necessary to commit the offence on the other. He went on to state that the attempt begins 'when the defendant embarks on the crime proper'.

▶ R v CAMPBELL [1991]

To be liable of a criminal attempt the defendant must have done an act that is more than merely preparatory.

Facts
The defendant was arrested close to the post office he intended to rob equipped with an imitation firearm that was not drawn.

Held
These acts did not equate to acts that were more than merely preparatory.

Mere preparation	Liability for attempt 'midway course'	The 'last act'
for example, buying the gun	taking aim	pulling the trigger

It seems that the courts take a relatively restricted view of what amounts to going beyond mere preparation. For example, in *R v Campbell* [1991], the defendant, who was armed with (but had not drawn) an imitation firearm, was arrested within a yard of the door of a post office which he intended to rob. Nevertheless, the Court of Appeal held that there was no evidence on which a jury could 'properly and safely' find that the defendant's acts were more than merely preparatory. Similarly, in *R v Geddes* [1996], another borderline case, the defendant was found in the boys' toilet of a school, equipped with lengths of string, sealing tape and a knife. He was charged and convicted of attempted false imprisonment, but successfully appealed. Although there was no doubt about the defendant's intention, it was held that the evidence showed no more than that he had made preparations, got himself ready and positioned himself ready to commit the offence. He had not had any contact with any potential victim, nor could it be said that he had moved from the role of preparation and planning into the area of execution or implementation. In short, there was no evidence that he did anything more than merely preparatory actions.

In *R v Tosti* [1997], the two accused had provided themselves with oxyacetylene equipment, driven to the scene of a planned burglary, concealed the equipment in a hedge, approached the door of a barn and examined the padlock on it. They then became aware that they were being watched and ran off. They were convicted of attempted burglary and their subsequent appeal was dismissed.

The distinction between *Geddes* and *Tosti* is that, in the former case, the evidence did not show that the defendant had made contact with a victim (that is, a child to imprison), whereas, in the latter, the accused had made contact with a target (that is, the barn to burgle). Presumably, it was when the accused started to 'examine' the padlock that they moved beyond planning and preparation to execution.

In *Bowles and Bowles* [2004] the defendants prepared a will, favouring themselves, for an elderly neighbour. They did not however execute it but left it in a drawer. Their conduct was deemed to be merely preparatory towards making a false instrument.

Mens rea

The general principle is that the defendant must have the *full* or specific intention to commit the offence in question (*R v Mohan* [1976]). For example, on a charge of attempted murder, intending to do GBH would not suffice; there must be an intention to kill. However, an indirect intention (foresight of consequence as a virtual certainty) was held to be sufficient in *R v Walker and Hayles* [1990]. In that case the defendants had threatened to kill the victim and dropped him from a third floor balcony. The convictions for attempted murder were upheld.

Impossibility

It is now clear that impossibility will be no defence to a charge of attempt.

In *R v Shivpuri* [1986] the defendant was found in possession of a suitcase containing bags of a white substance. He confessed to receiving and distributing what he assumed to be an illegally imported drug. The substance turned out not to be a prohibited drug but he was still guilty of an attempt to commit the relevant offences of dealing with and harbouring A and B class drugs.

Offences that can be attempted

Generally, any offence triable in England and Wales as an indictable offence (that is, any offence triable only on indictment, or triable either way) may be attempted (s 1(4) of the Criminal Attempts Act 1981).

However, the following offences cannot be attempted:

▨ statutory or common law conspiracy;

▨ offences of assisting an arrestable offender or compounding an arrestable offence contrary to s 4(1) and s 5(1) of the Criminal Law Act 1967;

▨ aiding, abetting, counselling or procuring the commission of an offence (s 1(4)(b) of the Criminal Attempts Act 1981).

Does impossibility negate liability?

Incitement	Yes
Conspiracy	No
Attempt	No

PARTICIPATION

One can be liable as a principal or as an accessory to an offence.

▨ *Principal*: the actual perpetrator of the offence.

▨ *Accessory*: one who aids, abets, counsels or procures the commission of the offence. Generally, liability as an accessory can arise in relation to any offence.

Section 8 of the Accessories and Abettors Act 1861 provides: 'Whosoever shall aid, abet, counsel, or procure the commission of [any offence], shall be liable to be tried, indicted, and punished as a principal offender.' Therefore the distinction between an accessory and a principal offender is of little importance in many cases.

Definition of accessorial liability: *actus reus*

In practice, the phrase 'aid, abet, counsel or procure' is commonly used as a whole without defining which of the four constituent words correctly encapsulates the defendant's conduct. However certain authorities have attempted to isolate the precise meanings of the words. Generally, 'aid' and 'abet' are considered to cover assistance and encouragement given at the time of the offence, whereas 'counsel' and 'procure' more often describe advice and assistance given at an earlier stage. The four modes of accessorial participation have also been differentiated in terms of requirements of causation and consensus (see table).

Action	Time	Causation required?	Consensus required?
Aiding, that is, helping	Before or during offence	Yes (1)	No
Abetting, that is, encouraging	During offence	No	Yes
Counselling, that is, encouraging or threatening	Before offence	Yes (2)	Yes
Procuring, that is, causing	Before offence	Yes (3)	No

(1) Causation is required in the sense that the defendant must assist the principal to commit the offence earlier, more easily or more safely.
(2) Counselling must have had some effect on the principal's mind.
(3) Direct causation required.

■ Procuring: there must be a causal link to the principal's act, but there is no requirement of consensus. For example, if a defendant secretly laces another person's drink, and that person is then subsequently convicted of drink driving, the defendant will be liable for procuring the offence in having brought it about, despite there being no meeting of minds (*AG's Ref (No 1 of 1975)*).

■ Counselling: requires less of a causal link. A person can counsel a principal who has already decided to commit the crime (*Gianetto* [1997]). It need only be shown that the counsellor had some effect on the principal's mind. However, there does need to be some meeting of minds in so far as the act done must be within the scope of the authority or advice given by the counsellor (*R v Calhaem* [1985]).

Mens rea

The requisite *mens rea* consists of (1) an *intention* to aid, abet, etc, and (2) knowledge of the crime the principal intends to commit.

Intention to aid does not require the defendant's purpose or motive to be that the principal offence should be committed. For example, Devlin J said in *National Coal Board v Gamble* [1959]:

> If one man deliberately sells to another a gun to be used for murdering a third, he may be indifferent about whether the third man lives or dies and interested only in the cash profit to be made out of the sale, but he can still be an aider and abettor. To hold otherwise would be to negative the rule that *mens rea* is a matter of intent only and does not depend on desire or motive.

Difficulties may arise in relation to *knowledge* where the offence is to be committed in the future or by a person of whose precise intentions the accused cannot be certain in advance. An example is where the defendant knows that a burglary is to be committed and provides equipment to be used in the burglary. He is guilty even if he does not know of the precise details of the proposed offence, provided that he knows the *type of crime* to be committed (*R v Bainbridge* [1960]).

Mere presence at the scene

There will be no intention to aid (or encourage) where the defendant was merely present at the scene of the crime and he did not personally appreciate the natural and probable consequences of his action. For example, in *R v Clarkson* [1971] two drunken soldiers entered a room to find other soldiers raping a woman and remained on the scene to watch. They were found not to have an intention to encourage. Obviously abetting or counselling will occur where a spectator applauds or purchases a ticket for an illegal performance (*Wilcox v Jeffery* [1951]).

Liability in cases of joint enterprise

Where individuals act together in the execution of a crime, it is clear that defendants may be charged as joint principals, for example where two individuals undertake an attack and one holds and the other stabs the victim.

However, difficulties have arisen in defining liability where individuals co-participate in a crime but in the course of committing the crime one of them goes beyond the scope of action intended by the others. In response, the courts have developed a doctrine of joint enterprise, particularly in relation to the offence of homicide.

This doctrine of joint enterprise has developed through a line of authorities and appears to have culminated in the twin-case decision of the House of Lords in *R v Powell and Daniel; R v English* [1997]. The doctrine states that an accomplice to a principal who kills can be guilty of murder if he foresees that the principal *might* kill or do GBH – he does not himself have to have the intention to kill or do GBH. Furthermore, the accomplice might not be present at the actual killing – he may be sitting in the getaway car or be in another part of the house; he may have hoped, and probably did hope, that the principal would not kill or do serious injury, however if the accomplice foresees the possibility that the principal might kill or do GBH as part of their joint enterprise, then he is liable to be convicted of murder. Therefore, an accomplice can be convicted of murder with a lesser degree of *mens rea* than the actual killer, who must have the *mens rea* himself to kill or do GBH.

▶ R v ENGLISH [1997]

An accomplice to a principal who kills can be guilty of murder if he foresees that the principal might kill or do GBH – he does not have to have the intention to kill or do GBH.

Facts
The defendant agreed to assault a police officer with wooden posts. During the attack the principal stabbed the officer to death. The defendant had no knowledge that the principal had brought a knife to the attack.

Held
Where the principal acts in a fundamentally different way to that foreseen by the defendant, the defendant will not be liable for murder as a secondary party.

However, even in cases where the accomplice foresees death or GBH, he may escape liability for murder where the principal offender causes death by an act fundamentally different from that foreseen:

Scenario 1

The accomplice does not contemplate the use of the weapon and the principal kills with a weapon (*R v Anderson and Morris* [1966]). However, if the principal produces a weapon and the accomplice continues to participate in the crime he will be liable (*R v Uddin* [1998]).

Scenario 2

The accomplice foresees the use of a non-deadly weapon (eg a baseball bat) and the principal elects to use a deadly weapon (eg a gun). In *R v Gamble* [1989] the accomplice escaped liability where he foresaw the use of a gun to 'kneecap' but the principal offenders proceeded to kill the victim. By contrast, if the weapon used is different from, but as dangerous as, that contemplated by the accomplice, he will not escape liability: for example if he contemplated the use of a knife and the principal uses a gun to kill.

A point that remains unresolved in this area of law is whether, having escaped liability for murder, the accomplice should be liable for manslaughter. In the major line of cases the answer appears to be no. In *R v Anderson and Morris* the accomplice foresaw an attack on the victim but not serious harm; he was unaware that the principal had a knife. The principal stabbed the victim to death. The court held that the accomplice should not be convicted of manslaughter since the principal completely departed from the common design. A similar approach was adopted in *R v English* [1997]. However, a conviction for manslaughter was upheld in *Stewart and Schofield* [1995] and in *R v Gilmour* [2000]. In *Gilmour* the accomplice drove the car for two principals who petrol bombed a house, killing three child occupants. The accomplice knew that the house was to be petrol bombed but had not foreseen that serious harm would ensue. By contrast, the principals had intent to do GBH. The Court of Appeal held that the accomplice could be found guilty of manslaughter on the basis that the principals carried out the very deed (*actus reus*) contemplated by the accomplice.

The fact that the accomplice had not foreseen serious harm meant that he could not be liable for murder, but nonetheless he had sufficient *mens rea* to be convicted of manslaughter. Cases such as *Anderson* and *English* were distinguished in that the principal offenders in those cases departed from the *actus reus* contemplated by the accomplice, whereas in *Stewart* and *Gilmour* the principals carry out the very act contemplated, albeit with greater *mens rea* than the accomplice.

Withdrawal from the common plan

What will amount to an effective withdrawal will depend upon which mode of participation the accomplice has engaged in. If the defendant has assisted or encouraged the commission of the offence prior to its commission, then it seems that all that is required is that the defendant clearly communicates his withdrawal from the common plan (*R v Grundy* [1977]; *R v Rook* [1993]).

Where the defendant aids or abets at the scene of the crime, then much more will be required in order to constitute an effective withdrawal. Indeed, in these circumstances, nothing less than physical intervention may be required (*R v Becerra and Cooper* [1975]). However, in the case of spontaneous, as opposed to pre-planned, violence, a participant can effectively withdraw from the joint enterprise without necessarily communicating that withdrawal to the other parties (*R v Mitchell* [1998]).

Where there is an issue as to whether there have been one or two incidents leading onto a fatal attack, the jury have to be satisfied that the fatal injuries were sustained when the joint enterprise was continuing and that a particular defendant was still acting within that joint enterprise (*R v O'Flaherty* [2004]).

Victims as accomplices

In *R v Tyrrell* [1894], a girl below the age of 16 was found not guilty of aiding and abetting a man to have unlawful sexual intercourse with her. The principle was that a defendant cannot incur liability as an accomplice if the offence in question is one that was designed to protect a class of people of which the defendant is a member.

Acquittal of the principal

If the principal is acquitted because he has not committed the *actus reus* of the offence in question, then the defendant will not be liable as an accomplice as there is no offence of assisting or encouraging (*Thornton v Mitchell* [1940]). However, even if the principal has not committed the *actus reus* of the full offence, he may still be liable for attempt. In these circumstances, the defendant could be liable for aiding and abetting the attempt.

If the principal is acquitted because he can avail himself of some defence which is not available to the defendant, there is nothing to prevent the conviction of the defendant as an accomplice (*R v Bourne* [1952]).

If the principal is acquitted because he lacks the *mens rea* or capacity for the crime in question, the defendant may still incur liability either as a principal who has acted through an innocent agent (*R v Michael* [1840]) or as an accomplice (*R v Cogan and Leak* [1975]; *DPP v K and C* [1997]).

	Accomplice liable?	
	Yes	No
Principal lacks *actus reus*		✓
Principal lacks *mens rea*	✓	
Principal lacks capacity	✓	
Principal has defence not available to accomplice	✓	
Accomplice is a victim		✓

You should now be confident that you would be able to tick all of the boxes on the checklist at the beginning of this chapter. To check your knowledge of Inchoate offences and participation why not visit the companion website and take the Multiple Choice Question test. Check your understanding of the terms and vocabulary used in this chapter with the flashcard glossary.

3

Non-fatal offences against the person

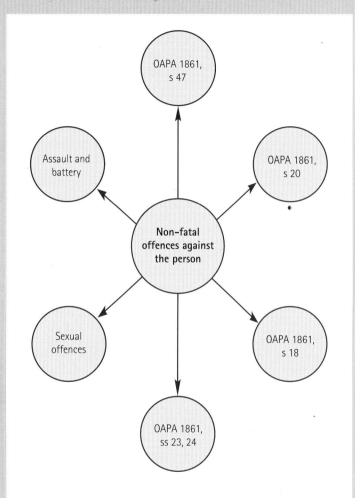

ASSAULT AND BATTERY

Actus reus

Assault and battery are separate summary offences.

The *actus reus* of an assault consists of causing the victim to apprehend immediate physical violence (*Logden v DPP* [1976]).

For many years, it was uncertain whether words alone could constitute an assault (*R v Meade and Belt* [1823]; *R v Wilson* [1955]). In *R v Burstow*; *R v Ireland* [1997], the House of Lords held that an assault could be committed by words alone, thus ending this longstanding uncertainty. The emphasis is now on the effect of the defendant's actions on the victim, rather than the means adopted by the defendant.

The *actus reus* of a battery consists of the actual infliction of unlawful physical violence. The degree of 'violence' required is minimal and can consist of the least touching of another (*Cole v Turner* [1705]).

Touching a person's clothing will amount to a battery, provided the contact is both unauthorised and capable of being felt by the victim (*R v Thomas* [1985]).

The courts presume that people impliedly consent to the normal touching that occurs in everyday life (*Collins v Wilcock* [1984]).

A battery can occur by indirect force where the defendant uses a weapon or other instrument to inflict physical harm on the victim such as a car (*Fagan v MPC* [1968]).

Also a battery may be caused by the indirect use of force. In *Haystead v CC of Derbyshire* [2000] the defendant punched the victim causing the victim to drop a baby she was holding. The defendant was convicted of battery on the baby.

Mens rea
The *mens rea* for both assault and battery is intention or recklessness.

Statutory offences
The Divisional Court in *DPP v Little* [1992] found that not only were common assault and battery separate offences, but also that the Offences Against the Person Act 1861 had put them into a statutory form. It is, therefore, no longer correct to refer to them as common law assault and battery. They should now be charged under s 39 of the Criminal Justice Act 1988.

SECTION 47 OF THE OFFENCES AGAINST THE PERSON ACT 1861

Definition

Section 47 of the Offences Against the Person Act 1861 provides that it is an offence to commit 'any assault occasioning actual bodily harm'.

Actus reus

An 'assault' within the meaning of s 47 can consist of either an assault in the technical sense of causing someone to fear immediate unlawful violence, or in the sense of a battery (that is, the infliction of unlawful violence).

'Occasioning' means the same as 'causing'; therefore, the rules relating to causation will be relevant. It will be remembered that the main test for establishing causation in law is to ask whether the result was a reasonably foreseeable consequence of what the defendant was doing (*R v Roberts* [1971]).

Actual bodily harm was defined in *R v Miller* [1954] so as to include any hurt or injury likely to interfere with the health or comfort of the victim. Minor cuts and bruises may suffice, though it normally reflects more serious injuries, such as broken teeth, extensive bruising or cuts which require medical treatment. However, in *T v DPP* [2003] it was held that the victim's momentary loss of consciousness, following a kick to the head, could properly be regarded as actual bodily harm, even where there was no other discernible evidence of injury. In *R v Chan-Fook* [1994], it was held that actual bodily harm includes psychiatric injury, but does not include mere emotions such as fear, distress or panic. The House of Lords, in *Burstow and Ireland* [1997], confirmed the decision in *Chan-Fook* by holding that recognisable psychiatric illness can amount to 'bodily harm' for the purposes of ss 47, 20 and 18 of the Offences Against the Person Act 1861. In *DPP v Smith* [2006] it was held that actual bodily harm included cutting off a woman's pony tail because it was part of the body. In *R v Morris* [1997], the Court of Appeal held that where a defendant is on a charge of an assault occasioning actual bodily harm and the harm is alleged to have been occasioned by a non-physical assault, the case should not go to the jury without expert psychiatric evidence.

Mens rea

Only the *mens rea* for assault or battery needs to be proven.

The *mens rea* is intention or recklessness. Either of these two mental states needs to be established only in relation to the initial assault; it is unnecessary to prove that the defendant intended or foresaw the risk of harm. In *R v Savage* [1992] the defendant intended to throw the contents of a beer glass over the victim, but unintentionally the glass slipped from her hand and caused a wounding to the victim. It was held that a conviction under s 20 (see below) could not be sustained without the defendant foreseeing the possibility of injury, but a conviction for an offence under s 47 was possible because the defendant intended to throw beer and this assault resulted in the victim's injury.

SECTION 20 OF THE OFFENCES AGAINST THE PERSON ACT 1861

Definition

Section 20 creates two offences of 'malicious wounding' and 'maliciously inflicting grievous bodily harm'.

Actus reus

A wounding requires a complete break of all the layers of the victim's skin (*JCC v Eisenhower* [1984]). Grievous bodily harm simply means 'serious harm' (*R v Saunders* [1985]).

Although most offences under s 20 will involve an assault, it was decided in *R v Wilson* [1983] that 'inflicting' does not necessarily imply an assault. It would seem that if 'inflicting' is to have any meaning at all it is to imply the need for causation. (See also *R v Burstow* [1997] where GBH, in the form of serious psychiatric injury, was inflicted by means of menacing telephone calls.)

Mens rea

The word 'malicious' implies a *mens rea* of intention or recklessness.

The decision of the court in *Mowatt* [1967] placed a 'gloss' on the *Cunningham* definition of recklessness in relation to s 20 in that the defendant must be shown to have been aware of the possibility of causing the victim *some physical harm*, albeit not serious harm.

As such foresight that the victim will be frightened is insufficient to find liability in relation to s 20; as stated above, the defendant must have foreseen some physical harm, if only of a minor character (*R v Sullivan* [1984]).

An intention to inflict a wound, not amounting to serious harm, would constitute sufficient *mens rea* for the s 20 offence, but not for the s 18 offence (see below).

SUMMARY OF NON-SEXUAL OFFENCES

See diagram on pp 46–7.

SECTION 18 OF THE OFFENCES AGAINST THE PERSON ACT 1861

Definition

By s 18, it is an offence to 'maliciously . . . wound or cause any grievous bodily harm . . . with intent to do some grievous bodily harm'.

Actus reus

The *actus reus* for this offence is exactly the same as that for the s 20 offence and consists of either a wound or grievous bodily harm.

Mens rea

This offence is a crime of intention only (*R v Belfon* [1976]). The meaning of intention is the same as it is for murder, therefore it includes both direct and oblique intention (*Bryson* [1985]).

Racially and religiously aggravated assaults

These aggravated features were added by the Crime and Disorder Act 1998. s 29 states that it is an offence if a person commits a common assault, s 47 or s 20 offence which is racially or religiously aggravated. If a defendant is convicted of this offence the maximum penalties they face are higher than the non-aggravated offences.

SECTIONS 23 AND 24 OF THE OFFENCES AGAINST THE PERSON ACT 1861

Actus reus

Both ss 23 and 24 require the administration of a noxious substance. Whether or not a substance is noxious will depend upon the circumstances in which it is taken. Such circumstances include the quality and quantity of the substance as well as the characteristics of the person to whom it is given (*R v Marcus* [1981]).

'Administering' means causing to be taken, for example, by spraying CS gas into someone's face (*R v Gillard* [1988]).

The *actus reus* of s 23 requires that life must be endangered or grievous bodily harm inflicted as a consequence of the administration of the noxious substance.

Mens rea

Both offences require that the noxious substance be administered intentionally or recklessly. In addition, s 24 requires proof of a further intent to injure, aggrieve or annoy the victim.

CONSENT

All the assaults above may only be criminal if the victim has not given their valid consent to the harm done. Not all consent given will be valid, for example no one can consent to their own murder and a child cannot consent to sexual intercourse.

One controversial issue arises around consent. What harm can a person consent to? In *AG's Reference* [1981] a quarrel between the victim and the defendant had led to a fist fight with the victim receiving injuries amounting to actual bodily harm. Lord Lane CJ surmised that consent cannot be a defence where actual bodily harm is either intended and or caused unless there was a good reason for it such as a medical procedure. This means that consent is no defence to offences under s 47, s 20 and s 18.

In *Brown* [1994] The House of Lords approved this position. The defendants were a group of sadomasochists who were convicted of offences under ss 47 and 20 for inflicting consensual pain to each other for sexual pleasure. The court was influenced in its decision by the fact that they could see no public interest in allowing people to indulge in such activities.

In *Wilson* [1996] the court did not follow *AG's Reference* and *Brown*. A husband was convicted of a s 47 offence for branding his wife's buttocks with a hot knife with her consent. His appeal against his conviction was allowed on the basis that this case involved consensual spousal activity and the level of harm was low. It would seem therefore that consent can still be a defence to the more minor forms of actual bodily harm.

SEXUAL OFFENCES

The Sexual Offences Act 2003 repealed almost all of the Sexual Offences Acts 1956 and 1967, the Indecency with Children Act 1960, and the Sex Offenders Act 1997. In their place it establishes a new law of rape and sexual assault, a new raft of sexual offences against vulnerable persons (children and the mentally disabled), a dramatically expanded range of offences dealing with prostitution, child pornography, sexual trafficking, and a number of completely new offences, including new crimes of voyeurism and 'grooming'.

Summary of non-sexual offences

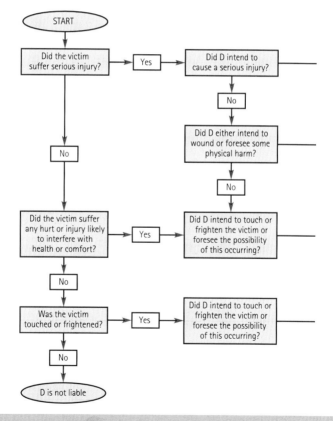

(1) RAPE

The offence of rape is defined in s 1 of the Sexual Offences Act (SOA) 2003.

Actus reus

The offence of rape can only be committed by a man as a principal offender (a woman or a man can be an accomplice to rape). It is an offence for a man to rape a woman or a man. The *actus reus* of the offence requires evidence of penile penetration of vagina, anus *or* mouth. There is no need to prove ejaculation.

Unlike those offences to which consent can be raised as a defence, rape requires the prosecution to prove the absence of consent as part of the *actus reus* of the offence. The significance of this is that the absence of consent has to be proved beyond reasonable doubt.

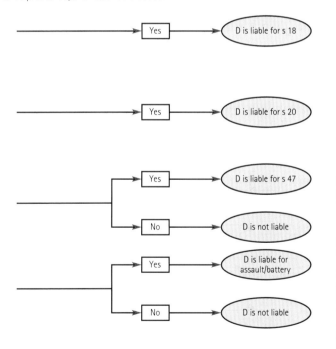

The SOA 2003 provides a limited definition of consent – 'a person consents if he agrees by choice, and has the freedom and capacity to make that choice' (s 74). This definition connotes a free, genuine and subsisting agreement, express or implied, to the act of sexual intercourse. So an agreement obtained by duress, not being a free agreement, does not amount to the 'consent' required. An agreement founded on the victim being mistaken or deceived as to the identity of the defendant, or as to the nature of the act, is not the 'consent' required, because it is not a genuine agreement. In *R v B* [2006] a defendant did not disclose to the complainant that he was HIV positive. He was not liable for rape as they had consensual sexual intercourse despite his non-disclosure.

Mens rea

The prosecution must show that the defendant intended to have sexual intercourse and that he did not *reasonably* believe that the victim was consenting (s 1(1)(c)). In other words, where the defendant claims he believed that the victim was consenting, if such a belief, though honestly held, is proved to be unreasonable, the jury should convict. In deciding whether the defendant's belief was unreasonable, the jury should have regard to all the circumstances, including any steps the defendant could reasonably have been expected to take to ascertain whether the victim consented (s 1(2)). This latter provision places an onus on the defendant to ascertain whether or not there is consent in situations where there might be doubt. As a whole, the burden on the Crown has clearly been lessened in that even if it cannot negative an honest belief that the victim was consenting, it may be able to show that that belief was unreasonable.

Presumptions about the absence of consent

In a further controversial development, the SOA 2003 introduces sets of presumptions about the absence of consent. The presumptions come in two forms:

▨ **Rebuttable presumptions (s 75)**

If it is proved that the defendant did the relevant act and one of the following circumstances existed at the time:

● violence was used against the complainant or the complainant was put in fear of immediate violence;

● the complainant was made to fear that violence was being used or would be used on another person (eg threats of violence towards complainant's child);

● the complainant was being unlawfully detained;

● the complainant was asleep;

● because of the complainant's disability, they would not have been able to communicate consent;

● a substance was administered to the complainant, without their consent, which was capable of causing the complainant to be stupefied or overpowered at the time of the relevant act,

it will be presumed that:

(a) the complainant did not consent to the act, and
(b) the defendant did not reasonably believe that the complainant consented,

unless the defendant adduces sufficient evidence to raise an issue to the contrary.

Conclusive presumptions (s 76)

The same presumptions will be also made if one of the following circumstances existed at the time:

● the defendant intentionally deceived the complainant as to the nature or purpose of the relevant act;

● the defendant intentionally induced the complainant to consent to the relevant act by impersonating a person known personally to the complainant.

But in these circumstances the presumptions will be conclusive: the defendant will have no opportunity to rebut them.

Other non-generic non-consensual offences

In relation to the other 'non-generic non-consensual' offences (namely assault by penetration (s 2), sexual assault (s 3) and causing a person to engage in sexual activity without consent (s 4)), the requirement that belief in consent is reasonable and the test as to what is reasonable, is the same as applies in relation to rape (s 1). Similarly, the rebuttable and conclusive presumptions as to consent also apply.

(2) ASSAULT BY PENETRATION

Section 2 covers assaults that involve penetration of the vagina or anus with objects or body parts other than the penis, or where the victim is not sure what was used to penetrate them. The penetration must be sexual so that it excludes, for example, intimate searches and medical procedures. Section 78 provides that an activity is 'sexual' if a 'reasonable' person would view it as such having regard to the nature of the act and where necessary to the circumstances and/or the purpose of any person in relation to the activity.

It must be proved that the penetration was intentional, that the victim did not consent to the penetration and that the defendant did not reasonably believe that the victim consented. This offence can be committed by a male or female, against a male or female. Assault by penetration and sexual assault together replace the old statutory offence of indecent assault.

(3) SEXUAL ASSAULT

Section 3 makes it an offence for the defendant intentionally to touch another person sexually without that person's consent, provided that the defendant does not reasonably believe that there is consent. This offence is intended to capture all other non-penetrative behaviour previously caught by the offence of indecent assault. 'Touching' is defined in the Act (s 79) so as to include touching (a) with any part of the body, (b) with anything else, (c) through anything, and includes touching amounting to penetration. This offence can be committed by a male or female, against a male or female.

(4) CAUSING A PERSON TO ENGAGE IN SEXUAL ACTIVITY WITHOUT CONSENT

Section 4 makes it an offence for a defendant intentionally to cause another person to engage in sexual activity without that person's consent. As above, if the defendant contends that he believed there was consent, the Crown must prove that he had no such belief, or, if he had, that his belief was unreasonable in the circumstances. This provision was intended to close a perceived gap in the law to allow the prosecution of someone who forces another person to perform sexual or indecent acts against their will, either on themselves (eg forcing another to masturbate) or on the offender (eg a woman who compels a man to penetrate her), or to engage in sexual activity with another person (eg forcing another to masturbate a third person). This offence can be committed by a male or female, against a male or female.

RAPE AND OTHER OFFENCES AGAINST CHILDREN UNDER 13 (ss 5–8)

A child under 13 cannot give consent. Therefore, in relation to the offences listed above (the 'non-generic' offences) the prosecution need only prove that the defendant did the relevant act. Whether or not the child consented is irrelevant.

By contrast, absence of consent (or a reasonable belief in consent) must still be proved by the prosecution in cases where the child is 13 or older. However, sexual intercourse with a child below 16 remains unlawful, even if the child willingly engages in the activity or even encourages it. Where a 13-, 14- or 15-year-old consents to the relevant act, the defendant would not fall to be charged under one of the non-generic non-consensual offences, that is, rape, assault by penetration, and so forth. However, the defendant will have committed one of the other child sexual offences.

Child sex offences (ss 9–15)

- Sexual activity with a child (s 9);

- causing or inciting a child to engage in sexual activity (s 10);

- engaging in sexual activity in the presence of a child (s 11);

- causing a child to watch a sexual act (s 12);

- meeting a child following sexual grooming etc (s 15).

A defendant will commit one of these offences if he engages in the relevant activity with a child under 16 and he does not reasonably believe that the child was 16. In other words, if the defendant contends that he believed that the child was 16, the Crown must prove that he had no such belief, or, if he had, that his belief was unreasonable in the circumstances. If the child was under 13, the offence will be made out regardless of what the defendant believed.

In all cases, whether or not the child consented to the activity is irrelevant.

OTHER OFFENCES AND PROVISIONS UNDER THE SEXUAL OFFENCES ACT 2003

The Act also covers offences involving an abuse of a position of trust towards a child, familial child sex offences, offences designed to give protection to persons with a mental disorder or a learning disability, offences relating to prostitution, child pornography, and trafficking. It provides for preparatory offences, such as administering a substance with intent to commit a sexual offence, and a number of miscellaneous offences, such as voyeurism and intercourse with an animal. There is provision for extra-territorial jurisdiction for most of the offences contained in the Act if committed against a child under 16.

Part 2 of the Act contains extensive provisions relating to registration and notification obligations imposed on sex offenders.

You should now be confident that you would be able to tick all of the boxes on the checklist at the beginning of this chapter. To check your knowledge of Non-fatal offences against the person why not visit the companion website and take the Multiple Choice Question test. Check your understanding of the terms and vocabulary used in this chapter with the flashcard glossary.

4

Fatal offences

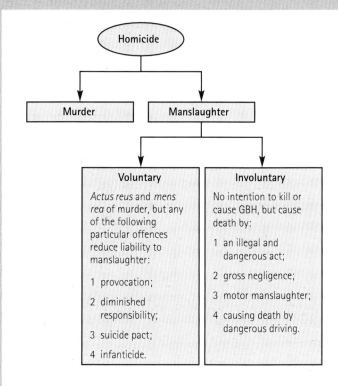

MURDER

Actus reus

The *actus reus* of murder is causing the unlawful death of a human being.

A patient kept alive on a life support machine is not regarded as legally dead and is, therefore, capable of being murdered. The original attacker will be held to have caused death if the machine is turned off as a result of a medical decision made in good faith (*R v Malcherek and Steel* [1981]).

The law of homicide protects the newborn child once it becomes capable of independent existence from the mother, and this includes a conjoined twin who is totally dependent on its twin for oxygenated blood (*Re A (Children) (Conjoined twins: surgical separation)* [2001]). There is no need for the umbilical cord to have been cut (*R v Reeves* [1839]), but the child must have been totally expelled from the mother's womb (*R v Poulton* [1832]).

Mens rea

The necessary *mens rea* for murder is an intention to kill or cause grievous bodily harm (*R v Vickers* [1957]).

In cases where it is not clear whether the defendant had such an intention, the jury must consider the evidence of what the defendant actually foresaw, and the more evidence there is that he foresaw death or grievous bodily harm as a consequence of his actions, the stronger the inference that he intended to kill (*R v Hancock and Shankland* [1986]).

In *R v Nedrick* [1986], the court supplemented the decision in *Hancock* by suggesting that the jury must be satisfied that the defendant foresaw death or grievous bodily harm as a virtual certainty before they could infer intention. The House of Lords, in *R v Woollin* [1998], confirmed the approach of the Court of Appeal in *Nedrick*, with the small modification that the more logical and simpler word 'find' should be used instead of 'infer'.

❱ R v WOOLLIN [1998]

Where a harm was the virtually certain result of the defendant's actions and the defendant appreciated such, a jury can find intention.

Facts
Woollin was convicted of murder after losing his temper and shaking his baby son and throwing him on a hard surface. The trial judge did not use the trial direction provided by *Nedrick* [1986].

Held
Intention can only be found where the jury are satisfied that the harm caused was a virtually certain consequence of the defendant's actions which the defendant appreciated.

Where the defendant's foresight of the harm was anything less than virtual certainty, they would lack intention.

Level of foresight		
Certainty	= ⎫	
Virtual certainty	= ⎬	Intention
Highly probable	= ⎫	
Probable	= ⎬	Recklessness
Zero	=	No *mens rea*

MANSLAUGHTER

VOLUNTARY MANSLAUGHTER

There are four particular defences that can operate to reduce a charge of murder to that of manslaughter: provocation, diminished responsibility, suicide pact and infanticide.

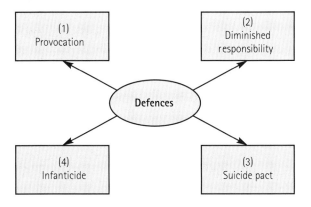

(1) PROVOCATION

Provocation existed as a common law defence prior to the Homicide Act 1957. At common law provocation was defined by Devlin J in *R v Duffy* [1949]:

Provocation is some act, or series of acts, done ... to the accused which would cause in any reasonable person, and actually causes in the accused, a sudden and temporary loss of self-control, rendering the accused so subject to passion as to make him or her for the moment not master of his mind.

Section 3 of the Homicide Act 1957 expanded on this, providing that:

Where on a charge of murder there is evidence on which a jury can find that the person charged was provoked (whether by things done or by things said or by both together) to lose his self-control, the question whether the provocation was enough to make a reasonable man do as he did shall be left to be determined by the jury; and in determining that question the jury shall take into account everything both done and said according to the effect which, in their opinion, it would have on a reasonable man.

This requires the prosecution to prove all the elements of murder *and* to disprove the provocation. The elements to the defence of provocation are:

(a) there must be some provocative conduct that causes

(b) the defendant to lose self-control and, if this is the case

(c) a reasonable person would also have lost self-control and done as the defendant did.

Conduct amounting to provocation

On the question of what can amount to provocation, it is no longer restricted to 'some act, or series of acts', since s 3, with the phrase 'whether by things done or by things said or by both together', clearly envisages that words alone can constitute provocation. In effect there is little legal restriction on what can cause provocation. However, a loss of self-control caused by fear, panic, sheer bad temper or circumstances (eg slow traffic due to snow) would not be enough (*R v Acott* [1997]).

Normally, provocation will be something done or said by the dead man to the defendant, but it need not necessarily be so; alternatively it may be something done to a third party (eg a loved one) or it may be something done by a third party (eg actions of a wife's lover might provoke a husband to kill his wife).

Loss of self-control

A further general rule is that that provocation must result in a 'sudden and temporary loss of self-control' and it should be distinguished from revenge. Where there is a significant time delay it is less likely to be a case of provocation, as it may be expected that the defendant has had time to reflect. For example, the defence failed in *R v Ibrams* [1981] where the defendant had been bullied and terrorised over a period but the last occasion of provocation was seven days before the planned fatal attack. However, provocation may be cumulative (eg in cases of battered woman syndrome), such that the final instance may be relatively minor but is 'the straw that breaks the camel's back'; nonetheless there must still be evidence that the defendant did actually lose self-control. See *R v Humphreys* [1995] and *R v Thornton (No 2)* [1996].

Two conditions

The courts have interpreted s 3 such that a jury is required to ask two questions in order to establish whether or not the defence of provocation is made out:

1 Was the defendant actually provoked to lose his self-control? And if so,
2 Given that provocation, would a reasonable man have reacted as the defendant did?

If the answer is yes to both questions the defence of provocation is available.

In considering the first question – sometimes described as the gravity of the provocation and said to be a *subjective test* – it is for the jury to take into account the personal characteristics of the defendant. For example, impotence, alcoholism or drug addiction may make a man more susceptible to taunts about his condition – taunts that might be meaningless to an 'ordinary' reasonable man.

On the second question – commonly referred to as the *objective test* – the issue has been more vexed. Until the decision of the House of Lords in *R v Smith (Morgan)* [2001], the leading authority of *DPP v Camplin* [1978] held that in relation to the objective test, personal characteristics other than sex or age must be excluded. Only in that way, it was argued, can the test of a reasonable man objectively regarded be applied; only in that way can a uniform assessment be made. Departures from that approach destroy the concept of a reasonable man by whose standard of control the behaviour of the particular individual is to be judged. However, in a gradual erosion of this objective principle, the Court of Appeal sought to 'graft' on to the reasonable man characteristics that were described as 'not wholly inconsistent' with the concept:

■ chronic post-traumatic stress disorder: *R v Ahluwalia* [1992];

■ eccentric and obsessive personality traits: *R v Dryden* [1995];

■ abnormal immaturity and attention-seeking: *R v Humphreys* [1995].

By contrast, the House of Lords appeared to reject any such erosion of the objective test. In a Privy Council decision, *Luc Thiet Thuan v R* [1996], Lord Goff criticised the Court of Appeal's approach, firstly, for its blurring of the line between diminished responsibility and provocation, and secondly, for the difficulties it raises for the jury in imagining the standards to be expected of a reasonable person with these grafted-on characteristics. It became clear through these cases that some characteristics may affect the defendant's ability to control themselves. Other characteristics could make the defendant more sensitive to the provocation. In this instance the gravity of the provocation would be greater to the defendant.

This distinction was lost in *R v Smith (Morgan)* [2001], a controversial House of Lords' decision. The defendant was suffering from clinical depression, which affected his abilities of self-control.

Rejecting the approach of Lord Goff in *Luc Thiet Thuan*, the Lords, in a bold and liberalising step, ruled that the relevant characteristics of the defendant can now be taken into account in relation to both subjective and objective tests. Thus a suitable direction after *Smith* might be summarised as follows:

Given all the circumstances was the defendant provoked such that he lost self-control? And if so, did the defendant's reaction measure up to the standard of self-control that can reasonably *be expected of him*?

The court, however, put certain limits upon the type of characteristics to be taken into account: simple pugnacity, or a tendency to violent rages or childish tantrums should be disregarded. Given that this is a bold expansion of the defence, it may be that the courts will put further limits upon what can qualify as a 'characteristic' to be taken into account.

In *R v Weller* [2004] the Court of Appeal interpreted the majority speeches in *Smith* to mean that no aspect of a person's character should be ignored when considering what standard of self-control is to be reasonably expected of them. Therefore characteristics such as jealousy remained as matters which fell for consideration in connection with the second, objective element of provocation.

However the decision in *Smith* must now be reviewed in the light of the Privy Council case of *Attorney General for Jersey v Holley* [2005] in which an enlarged board of nine Law Lords held on a majority of six to three that the majority decision in *Smith* had been erroneous. The Board rejected the adoption of a flexible standard which permitted a jury to take account of the defendant's particular abnormalities in assessing the objective element and approved instead the approach taken in *Luc Thiet Thuan*. In the case the board held that the defendant's disease of alcoholism was not to be taken into account in the jury's determination of what standard of self-control could be expected of him.

▶ ATTORNEY-GENERAL FOR JERSEY v HOLLEY [2005]

Factors that effect the defendant's ability to exercise self-control will not be considered for the defence of provocation.

Facts
The defendant was a chronic alcoholic who killed his wife whilst intoxicated. He argued that his illness should be a characteristic taken into account for the defence of provocation.

Held
Characteristics that affect the gravity of the provocation to the defendant can be considered, but factors, such as alcoholism, that effect the defendant's ability to exercise self-control cannot.

The Court of Appeal ruled in *James and Karimi* [2006] that the Privy Council in Holley is good law and overrules the House of Lords in *Smith*.

(2) DIMINISHED RESPONSIBILITY

This defence is purely statutory. Section 2(1) of the Homicide Act 1957 provides:

Where a person kills or is a party to the killing of another, he shall not be convicted of murder if he was suffering from such abnormality of mind (whether arising from a condition of arrested or retarded development of mind or any inherent causes or induced by disease or injury) as substantially impaired his mental responsibility for his acts and omissions in doing or being a party to the killing.

The burden is on the defendant to prove the defence on the balance of probabilities (*R v Dunbar* [1957]). In *R v Byrne* [1960], Lord Parker CJ defined abnormality of mind as 'a state of mind that the reasonable person would find abnormal'. In the case, Byrne, a sexual psychopath who found it difficult to control his perverted desires, came within s 2. This is considerably wider than the 'defect of reason' under the *M'Naghten* rules (see insanity in Chapter 6). If it is established that the defendant has abnormality of the mind, it must also be shown that such abnormality impaired his 'mental responsibility'.

Does alcoholism found a defence within s 2? This was considered in *R v Tandy* [1989]. An alcoholic strangled her 11-year-old daughter after drinking a bottle of vodka and upon hearing that the daughter had been sexually abused. The Court of Appeal upheld her conviction for murder, and in doing so they indicated that the defence based on alcoholism was only available in two circumstances:

- where the alcoholism is so chronic that the brain has been injured by repeated abuse such that there is gross impairment of the defendant's judgment and emotional response;

- where the alcoholism has reached a level where although the brain has not been damaged to the extent just stated, nonetheless the addiction is so severe that the defendant is no longer able to resist the impulse to drink, in effect making the defendant's drinking an involuntary act.

By contrast, if the defendant simply does not resist an impulse to drink and this drinking brings about the impairment of mental responsibility, then the defence of diminished responsibility will not be available to the defendant.

Where a defendant seeks to rely on an abnormality of the mind other than alcoholism (eg clinical depression) to establish a defence under s 2, but is intoxicated at the time of the killing, it had previously been thought that the defendant had to show that he would have killed even if he had been sober before he could rely on the defence (*R v Atkinson* [1985]). This was overruled by the House of Lords in *R v Dietschmann* [2003] and it is now established that the defendant's abnormality is not required to be the sole cause of the conduct. The Lords ruled that where a defendant is intoxicated at the time of the killing and seeks to prove diminished responsibility on the basis of an abnormality of the mind other than alcoholism, he need only show that his abnormality of mind substantially impaired his mental responsibility. It does not matter that intoxication was an additional contributory factor or that he may not have killed without being drunk.

(3) SUICIDE PACT

Section 4 of the Homicide Act 1957 provides that any killing carried out in pursuance of a suicide pact will be treated as manslaughter, rather than as murder.

(4) INFANTICIDE

Section 1(1) of the Infanticide Act 1938 provides that, where a woman kills her child before it reaches the age of 12 months and there is evidence to show that at the time of the killing the balance of her mind was disturbed by the effect of giving birth, then the jury is entitled to find her guilty of infanticide rather than murder.

INVOLUNTARY MANSLAUGHTER

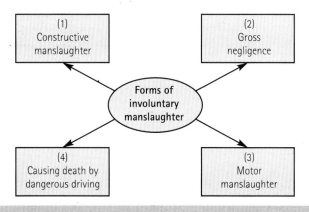

(1) CONSTRUCTIVE MANSLAUGHTER

This offence requires proof that the defendant intentionally committed a dangerous criminal act which resulted in the death of the victim. *DPP v Newbury and Jones* [1976] confirmed the four elements of the offence as:

(a) defendant did an act with the intention to do so;

(b) the act was criminally unlawful;

(c) the act was dangerous; and

(d) the act caused the victim's death.

The objective nature of the 'dangerous' act was established in *R v Church* [1966], where it was said that:

> ... the unlawful act must be such as all sober and reasonable people would inevitably recognise must subject the other person to, at least, the risk of some harm ...

What is meant by 'harm' in this context was clarified in *R v Dawson* [1985], where it was held that the jury must be directed to consider the possibility of *physical* harm as opposed to mere emotional disturbance.

Moreover, the reasonable person should be endowed with all the knowledge that the defendant has gained in the course of the crime (*R v Watson* [1989]).

The illegal act required for constructive manslaughter must be a criminal act (*R v Franklin* [1883]), but there is no need for the act to be 'aimed' at the victim. For example, in *R v Goodfellow* [1986] the defendant, wishing to be rehoused, set fire to his council house. The fire spread faster than he expected, killing his wife, child, and another person. The Court of Appeal upheld the conviction for manslaughter, even though the defendant's acts were not directed at the victims but rather against property.

It follows that any act which is both dangerous and criminal will be capable of forming the *actus reus* of the offence. All that is required for the *mens rea* is an intention to do such an act; it is not necessary for the defendant to know that the act is criminal or dangerous (*DPP v Newbury and Jones* [1976]).

(2) KILLING BY GROSS NEGLIGENCE

Following the decision of the House of Lords in *R v Adomako* [1994], to establish this form of manslaughter the prosecution must prove:

■ *A duty of care*

It is submitted that the concept of a duty of care, obviously borrowed from the law of tort, is unlikely to prove problematic in the context of criminal law.

■ *Breach of that duty*

The duty may be breached whenever there is a reasonably foreseeable risk of injury to health occurring (*R v Stone and Dobinson* [1977]).

■ *Gross negligence*

According to the Court of Appeal in *R v Prentice and Others* [1993], a decision confirmed by the House of Lords in *R v Adomako*, any of the following states of mind could lead a jury to make a finding of gross negligence:

(a) indifference to an obvious risk of injury to health;
(b) actual foresight of the risk coupled with the determination nevertheless to run it;
(c) an appreciation of the risk coupled with an intention to avoid it, but also coupled with such a high degree of negligence in the attempted avoidance as the jury considers justifies conviction;
(d) inattention or failure to advert to a serious risk which goes beyond 'mere inadvertence' in respect of an obvious and important matter which the defendant's duty demanded he should address.

Two of the above four types of gross negligence, (a) and (b), seem to be subjective mental states (in relation to (a), surely, you can only be *indifferent* to a result which is foreseen?), whereas (c) and (d) are clearly objective mental states. However, each case, it seems, is subject to the overriding judgment of the jury: '. . . gross negligence which the jury consider justifies criminal conviction . . .'.

A company can be convicted of corporate manslaughter based on killing by gross negligence, but only where there is evidence establishing the guilty mind of an identified human individual for the same crime – that individual must be an employee senior enough to be regarded as the directing mind and will of the company (*AG's Reference (No 2 of 1999)* [2000]).

(3) MOTOR MANSLAUGHTER

The *actus reus* of this common law offence consists of driving in such a manner as to cause the death of another road user.

In *Adomako*, the House of Lords, overruling the earlier decision of the House in *R v Seymour* [1983], held that gross negligence was the proper *mens rea* for this offence. Lord Mackay stated that motor manslaughter charges should be reserved not only for the most culpable instances of negligence, but also for cases where the breach of duty brought with it a risk, not merely of injury or damage (as with the statutory offence – see below), but of death. It seems that, for manslaughter involving motor vehicles, what is required is driving so far below that of the reasonable driver as to be not only dangerous, but *inherently life threatening*.

(4) CAUSING DEATH BY DANGEROUS DRIVING

Causing death by dangerous driving, defined in s 1 and s 2A of the Road Traffic Act 1988 is, in effect, causing death by grossly negligent driving.

This is because the defendant's driving must fall *far below* the standard of the reasonably competent driver.

It must be obvious to the careful and competent driver that driving in the way that the defendant was actually driving would cause danger of injury to the person or serious damage to property.

SUMMARY

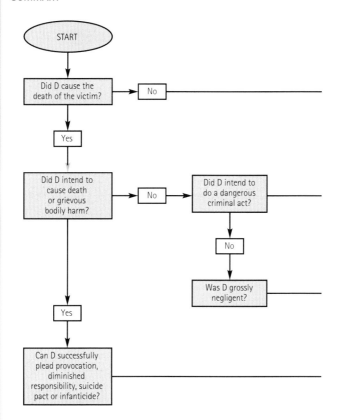

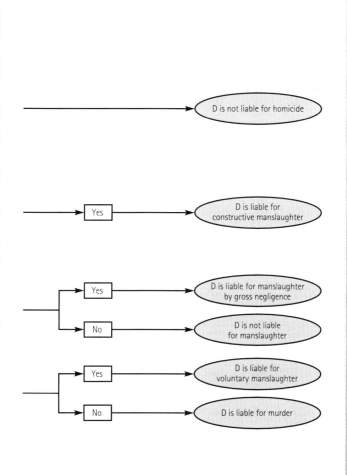

You should now be confident that you would be able to tick all of the boxes on the checklist at the beginning of this chapter. To check your knowledge of Fatal offences why not visit the companion website and take the Multiple Choice Question test. Check your understanding of the terms and vocabulary used in this chapter with the flashcard glossary.

5

Offences against property

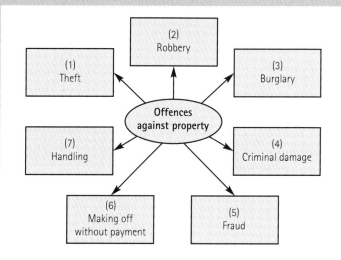

(1) THEFT

Definition

The basic definition of theft is to be found in s 1(1) of the Theft Act 1968, which provides that a person who:

> ... dishonestly appropriates property belonging to another with the intention of permanently depriving the other of it ...

is guilty of theft.

Relevant sections of Theft Act 1968

Dishonestly	appropriates	property	belonging to another	with the intention of permanently depriving the other of it
s 2	s 3	s 4	s 5	s 6

Actus reus

Property

Section 4(1) of the Theft Act 1968 defines 'property' as:

> . . . money and all other property, real or personal, including things in action and other intangible property.

This seemingly all-encompassing definition is subject to both common law and statutory exceptions. The following do not constitute property:

- information (*Oxford v Moss* [1979]);

- electricity (*Low v Blease* [1975]);

- a human corpse (*R v Sharpe* [1857]);

- land (s 4(2));

- wild plants (s 4(3));

- wild animals (s 4(4)).

However, there are also some exceptions to the exceptions, rendering some of the above capable of being stolen in certain circumstances:

- a human corpse does become property capable of being stolen if skill or effort has been exercised on it (*Doodeward v Spence* [1907]); moreover, products of the body, such as blood and urine, are capable of being stolen (*R v Rothery* [1976]; *R v Welsh* [1974]). In *R v Kelly* [1998], the Court of Appeal held that human body parts are capable of being the subject of a charge of theft if they have acquired different attributes by virtue of the application of skill, such as dissection or preservation techniques;

- land can be appropriated by (a) a trustee, personal representative or liquidator; (b) someone not in possession can appropriate anything severed from the land; and (c) a tenant can appropriate any fixture (s 4(2)(a), (b) and (c));

- wild plants can be stolen if the whole plant is taken or the plant is taken for sale or reward (s 4(3));

■ wild animals can be stolen if they are tamed or ordinarily kept in captivity or have been, or are in the process of being, reduced into another's possession (s 4(4)).

Belonging to another

The basic definition of 'belonging to another' is contained in s 5(1) of the Theft Act 1968:

> Property shall be regarded as belonging to any person having possession or control of it, or having in it any proprietary right or interest . . .

Thus, in *R v Turner No 2* [1971], an owner was convicted of theft of his car when he removed it from a garage where it was undergoing repairs without informing the proprietor. Since the garage had possession and control, the car was treated as if it belonged to another in accordance with s 5(1).

Section 5(3) of the Theft Act 1968 extends the meaning of 'belonging to another':

> Where a person receives property from or on account of another, and is under an obligation to the other to retain and deal with that property or its proceeds in a particular way, the property or proceeds shall be regarded (as against him) as belonging to another.

As the 'obligation' must be legally enforceable (*R v Gilks* [1972]), this will normally involve either contractual obligations or obligations imposed under a statute.

The terms of the contractual or statutory duty must be examined in order to establish the precise nature of the obligation. If the defendant is permitted to do what he likes with the property, his only obligation being to account in due course for an equivalent sum, s 5(3) does not apply (*R v Hall* [1973]). However, the defendant need not be under an obligation to retain particular monies; it is sufficient that he is under an obligation to keep in existence a fund equivalent to that which he has received (*Lewis v Lethbridge* [1987]).

It would appear that s 5(3) will apply where someone contracts on the basis that the money he hands over will be transferred by the recipient to a stake-holder or trustee. The recipient is under an obligation to deal with the money in a particular way and, if he dishonestly appropriates it, can be convicted of theft (*R v Kilneberg and Marsden* [1998]).

Section 5(4) covers the situation where the defendant receives property by mistake:

> Where a person gets property by another's mistake, and is under an obligation to make restitution ... then ... the property or proceeds shall be regarded (as against him) as belonging to the person entitled to restoration ...

Possible situations:

- mistaken overpayment of wages (*AG's Reference (No 1 of 1983)* [1984]);

- mistaken crediting of a bank account (*R v Shadrokh-Cigari* [1988]).

In addition, it is thought that the sub-section would apply to situations where the defendant receives too much change or too many goods by mistake.

Appropriation

Appropriation is defined in s 3(1) of the Theft Act 1968 as 'any assumption by a person or the rights of an owner'.

Appropriation can, therefore, take many forms, including:

- offering the property for sale (*R v Pitham and Hehl* [1976]);

- taking the property;

- pledging the property;

- destroying (although not damaging) the property;

- fixing the price of the property (*R v Morris* [1983]).

In *R v Gomez* [1993], the House of Lords decided that any interference with property belonging to another would amount to an appropriation, irrespective of whether the owner consented or authorised the act in question.

▶ R v GOMEZ [1993]

Property can be appropriated with or without the owner's consent and only one right of the owner need be assumed.

Facts
The defendant was charged with theft after wittingly deceiving his manager into believing cheques given for goods from a rogue were good.

Held
It was irrelevant that the owner had consented to the goods changing ownership, any interference with property belonging to another would amount to appropriation. Obviously for the offence of theft to be complete the relevant *mens rea* is also required.

As *Gomez* was a case where, on the facts, consent was obtained by fraud, it was thought that its *ratio* could be restricted to such cases. However, in *R v Hinks* [2000], the House of Lords held that the defendant could be guilty of theft even though the property had been validly transferred to her in the form of a gift. The House of Lords rejected arguments that the word 'appropriate' should be interpreted as if the word 'unlawfully' preceded it. The result is that everything depends on the defendant's state of mind, in particular whether or not the defendant is dishonest.

Mens rea

Dishonesty
There is a negative definition of dishonesty set out in s 2(1) of the Theft Act 1968. A person is not dishonest if he appropriates in the honest belief that:

■ he has a legal right to deprive another of the property (s 2(1)(a));

■ he would have the other's consent if the other knew of the appropriation and the circumstances of it (s 2(1)(b));

■ the person to whom the property belongs cannot be discovered by taking reasonable steps (s 2(1)(c)).

A positive test for establishing dishonesty was laid down by the Court of Appeal in *R v Ghosh* [1982]. In cases of doubt, the jury should be given the following direction:

> Was the defendant dishonest according to the standards of ordinary decent people? If yes, did the defendant realise that what he was doing was dishonest by these standards?

Intention to permanently deprive

In the vast majority of cases, it will be obvious whether or not the defendant had an intention to permanently deprive the other of the property at the moment of appropriation. However, in two situations, the defendant will be deemed to have such an intention to permanently deprive:

- if it is his intention 'to treat the thing as his own to dispose of regardless of the other's rights: and a borrowing or lending of it may amount to so treating it if, but only if, the borrowing or lending is for a period and in circumstances making it equivalent to an outright taking or disposal' (s 6(1)); or

- where he parts with property 'under a condition as to its return which he may not be able to perform' (s 6(2)).

In relation to s 6(1), the intention to permanently deprive will be deemed to exist if the defendant intended to return the goods in a fundamentally changed state so that virtually all of their value would have been lost (*R v Lloyd* [1985]). Similarly, someone who deals with property knowing that he is doing so in a way which risks its loss may be intending to 'treat the thing as his own to dispose of regardless of the other's rights' and may, therefore, be deemed to have an intention to permanently deprive under s 6(1) (*R v Fernandes* [1995]).

In *R v Marshall, Coombes and Eren* [1998], it was held that someone who buys an Underground ticket from a passenger and sells it on could be guilty of theft by virtue of s 6(1).

(2) ROBBERY

Definition

Section 8(1) of the Theft Act 1968 provides that:

> A person is guilty of robbery if he steals and immediately before or at the time of doing so, and in order to do so, he uses force on any person or puts or seeks to put any person in fear of being then and there subjected to force.

Actus reus

Force

As can be seen from the above definition, the Act requires proof of either the use or the threat of force against the person. Whether force actually has been used or threatened is a matter for the jury to decide (*R v Dawson* [1976]).

The force can be used or threatened against any person, not necessarily the owner of the property (*Smith v Desmond Hall* [1965]).

It is clear that the force or threat of force must occur before or at the time of stealing. The use of force even seconds after the appropriation has taken place would not amount to robbery. However, the courts have been prepared on some occasions to hold that an appropriation could consist of a continuing act (*R v Hale* [1978]).

Stealing

All the elements required for s 1(1) theft are necessary to establish that the defendant has stolen for the purposes of robbery. Thus, in *R v Robinson* [1977], the defendant's conviction for robbery was quashed on the basis that, since he honestly believed that he was entitled to the property in question, he was not dishonest under s 2(1)(a) and, therefore, was incapable of committing theft.

(3) BURGLARY

Definitions

Section 9 of the Theft Act 1968 creates two burglary offences.

Section 9(1)(a)

By s 9(1)(a), a person is guilty of burglary if 'he enters any building or part of a building as a trespasser' with an intention to:

- steal;
- inflict grievous bodily harm;

■ commit unlawful damage to the building or anything therein.

Note that s 63 of the Sexual Offences Act 2003 introduces a new offence of *trespass with intent to commit a sexual offence*, which replaces and expands on the old offence of entering as a trespasser with intent to rape (previously charged under s 9(1)(a)).

Section 9(1)(b)

A person is guilty of this offence if, having entered a building or part of a building as a trespasser, he steals or attempts to steal or inflict grievous bodily harm.

Actus reus

Both burglary offences require that the defendant has entered a building or part of a building as a trespasser.

Building or part of a building

In the Act there is no complete definition of what constitutes a 'building'. The following points should be noted in this respect:

■ inhabited vehicles or vessels will amount to a 'building' for the purposes of the Act, even when the inhabiting person is not there;

■ in *Stevens v Gourley* [1859], it was stated that a building was 'a structure of considerable size and intended to be permanent or at least to endure for a considerable length of time';

■ in *B and S v Leathley* [1979], a large freezer container without wheels and which was connected to the electricity supply was held to constitute a building;

■ in *Norfolk Constabulary v Seekings and Gould* [1986], a lorry trailer with wheels, used for storage and connected to the electricity supply, was held not to be a building;

■ in *R v Walkington* [1979], a customer who went behind a till counter was held to enter part of a building as a trespasser.

Entry

Section 9 requires that the defendant must enter, or have entered, a building or part of a building. In *R v Collins* [1972], it was held that an entry must be 'effective and substantial'.

In *R v Brown* [1985], a case which involved the defendant leaning through a broken shop window, it was held that the crucial word in the *Collins* test was 'effective' and that 'substantial' did not materially assist in the matter. As the defendant was able to reach the articles he wished to steal, his entry was held to be 'effective' and the conviction was upheld.

Similarly, in *R v Ryan* [1995], a defendant who had his head and arm trapped inside a building by a window was held to have entered for the purposes of burglary. In the light of *Brown* and *Ryan*, it seems that the courts are adopting a very broad approach to the 'effective' and/or 'substantial' test established in *Collins*.

As a trespasser

The defendant must not only enter a building, he must do so as a trespasser. A trespasser is someone who enters property without express or implied permission.

A defendant who has permission to enter for particular purposes, but then exceeds the express or implied conditions of entry, will enter as a trespasser. For example, in *R v Smith and Jones* [1976], the defendants had permission to enter the house of Smith's father for normal domestic purposes, but not in order to steal the television set.

The defendant must know or be reckless as to whether his entry is trespassory (*R v Collins* [1972]).

(4) CRIMINAL DAMAGE

Definitions

Section 1(1) Criminal Damage Act 1971

This sub-section provides that the 'basic' offence of criminal damage is committed where:

> A person who without lawful excuse destroys or damages any property belonging to another, intending to destroy or damage any such property or being reckless as to whether any such property would be destroyed or damaged.

Section 1(2)

This sub-section states that an 'aggravated' offence is committed where:

A person who without lawful excuse destroys or damages any property, whether belonging to himself or another:

(a) intending to destroy or damage any property or being reckless as to whether any property would be destroyed or damaged; and

(b) intending by the destruction or damage to endanger the life of another or being reckless as to whether the life of another would be thereby endangered.

Section 1(3)

This sub-section provides that where property is destroyed or damaged by fire, the offence is charged as arson and is punishable with a maximum sentence of life imprisonment.

Actus reus

Property

Property is defined in s 10(1) as anything of 'a tangible nature, whether real or personal, including money'.

Although somewhat similar to the definition of 'property' provided in s 4 of the Theft Act 1968, it should be noted that criminal damage can be committed in relation to land: while land cannot be stolen, conversely, intangible property can be stolen, but cannot be the subject of criminal damage.

Belonging to another

The property must belong to another for the purposes of s 1(1), but need not belong to another in relation to the s 1(2) offence.

Property will be treated as 'belonging to another' for the purposes of s 1(1) if that other has custody or control of it or has any proprietary right or interest in it or has a charge on it (s 10(2)).

Damage

Whether property has been destroyed or damaged will depend upon the circumstances of each case, the nature of the article and the way in which it is affected. The following cases provide illustrations of acts which were held to have amounted to criminal damage:

- in *Blake v DPP* [1993], a biblical quotation written on a concrete pillar with a marker pen was held to amount to criminal damage;

- similarly, in *Hardman and Others v Chief Constable of Avon and Somerset Constabulary* [1986], the spraying of human silhouettes by CND supporters on pavements was held to constitute criminal damage notwithstanding that the figures would be washed away by the next rainfall;

- in *Roe v Kingerlee* [1986], it was held that the application of mud to the walls of a cell could amount to damage as it would cost money to remove it;

- the unauthorised dumping of waste on a building site which cost £2,000 to remove was held to constitute criminal damage in *R v Henderson and Battley* [1984];

- in *Samuel v Stubbs* [1972], criminal damage was held to have been done to a policeman's helmet when it had been jumped upon causing a 'temporary functional derangement'.

The following two cases illustrate actions which were not held to have amounted to criminal damage:

- in *A (A Juvenile) v R* [1978], a football supporter who spat on a policeman's coat was found not to have committed criminal damage since the coat did not require cleaning or other expenditure;

- a scratch caused to a scaffolding bar did not amount to criminal damage in *Morphitis v Salmon* [1990] since its value or usefulness was not impaired.

Mens rea

The 'basic' s 1(1) offence

The *mens rea* required for the basic offence of criminal damage is an intention to do an act which would cause damage to property belonging to another or being reckless in relation to such an act.

In *R v G* [2004] recklessness for the purposes of the 1971 Act was defined as follows:

A person acts recklessly within the meaning of section 1 of the Criminal Damage Act 1971 with respect to:

> (i) a circumstance when he is aware of a risk that it exists or will exist;
>
> (ii) a result when he is aware of a risk that it will occur;
>
> and it is, in the circumstances known to him, unreasonable to take the risk.

The previous definition of recklessness propounded by the majority in *R v Caldwell* [1982] is no longer good law.

The 'aggravated' s 1(2) offence

The *mens rea* for this more serious form of criminal damage consists of an intention to damage property and an intention that the damaged property endanger life, or recklessness as to whether this occurs.

There is no need for life to actually be endangered. All that is required is that the defendant intended the damage to endanger life, or was reckless as to whether this occurred (*R v Dudley* [1989]).

However, the defendant's *mens rea* as to whether life is endangered must extend to the consequences of the criminal damage and not be limited merely to the act causing the damage. For example, in *R v Steer* [1980], the defendant's conviction under s 1(2) for firing rifle shots at the windows of his victim's house was quashed on appeal. There was no evidence that he intended or was reckless as to whether the broken glass, as opposed to the shots themselves, would endanger life.

Defences

Honest belief in the owner's consent is a defence under s 5(2)(a), which provides that a person will have a lawful excuse if:

> . . . he believed that the person or persons whom he believed to be entitled to consent to the destruction of or damage to the property in question has so consented, or would have so consented to it if he or they had known of the destruction or damage and its circumstances.

Defence of property

Under s 5(2)(b), the defendant will have a lawful excuse if, in order to protect property, he damaged other property provided he believed that the property was in immediate need of protection and that the means of protection were reasonable in the circumstances.

Section 5(3) clearly provides that the defendant's belief that his actions are reasonable does not itself have to be reasonable. However, the courts have sometimes appeared reluctant to judge defendants on the basis of what they considered to be reasonable in the circumstances (see *Blake v DPP* [1993]).

(5) FRAUD

Prior to the Fraud Act 2006 the offences involving deception were very technical and covered two Theft Acts. The law explained below was particularly complex. These offences have now been abolished by s 1 Fraud Act 2006.

See diagram opposite.

(a) Obtaining property by deception

Definition
Section 15(1) of the Theft Act 1968 provided:

> A person who by any deception dishonestly obtains property belonging to another, with the intention of permanently depriving the other of it, shall . . . be liable . . .

Actus reus

Property belonging to another
Section 34(1) provided that s 4(1) and s 5(1) relating to property belonging to another should apply generally for the purposes of the Act. The concepts of 'property' and 'belonging to another', therefore, have a similar meaning to that already noted in relation to s 1 theft.

Obtaining
Section 15(2) provided:

> For the purposes of this section a person is to be treated as obtaining property if he obtains ownership, possession or control of it and 'obtains' includes obtaining for another or enabling another to obtain or to retain.

Offences of deception

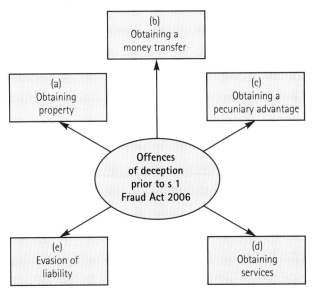

Clearly, the *actus reus* of the offence will be committed where the defendant induces the victim to sell, give or loan property. However, it seems that the offence would not be committed where the defendant by deception is allowed to retain property of which he already had possession or control. The appropriate charge in these circumstances would be one of theft, by virtue of s 3(1).

However, following the decision in *R v Gomez* [1993], that consent is irrelevant to appropriation, there would now seem to be a large area of overlap between s 1 and s 15.

Section 15(4) provided:

> For the purposes of this section 'deception' means any deception (whether deliberate or reckless) by words or conduct as to fact or as to law, including a deception as to the present intentions of the person using the deception or any other person.

Obviously, to constitute a deception, the statement must be untrue (*R v Deller* [1952]). Moreover, a statement of mere opinion cannot amount to a deception.

A deception can only work on a human mind, so a machine cannot be deceived (*Davies v Flackett* [1972]).

Clearly, conduct can amount to a deception (*DPP v Ray* [1974]). A defendant may also deceive by remaining silent where he is aware of a material change in circumstances (*R v Rai* [2000]).

Causation

The deception must be operative, in the sense that it must cause the obtaining of the property. It follows that the 'but for' test and other rules relating to causation, noted above, are relevant to deception.

In *R v Collis-Smith* [1971], the defendant, having filled his car with petrol, falsely told a garage attendant that his employer would pay. On appeal, it was held that the deception could not have been operative since it was not made until *after* the property in the petrol had already passed to the defendant. The appropriate charge in these circumstances would have been under s 2 of the Theft Act 1978 (see below).

Mens rea

The *mens rea* for the s 15 offence consists of three elements:

■ intention or recklessness in relation to the deception;

■ dishonesty;

■ intention to permanently deprive.

Both the *Ghosh* test and the s 6 provisions relating to an intention to permanently deprive apply to the s 15 offence. However, the s 2(1) negative definitions of dishonesty do not apply.

The problem posed by *Preddy*

In *Preddy* [1996], the House of Lords held that, although the appellants had obtained mortgages by giving false information, the transfer of money between bank accounts did not constitute an offence of obtaining property by deception. Although the effect is exactly the same as if the defendants had obtained property belonging to the victim, since the victim's account is debited and the defendant's account is credited, in law, nothing which formerly belonged to the victim now belongs to the defendant. A chose in action belonging to the victim has been diminished or extinguished and a different chose in action belonging to the defendant has been enlarged or created.

Not only does a money transfer, such as that which took place in *Preddy*, not fall within the ambit of s 15, it also does not constitute theft, since there is no appropriation by the defendant (*R v Caresana* [1996]). Of course, if the defendant has direct control of the victim's bank account and he dishonestly causes transfers to be made from it, there is a theft (*R v Hilton* [1997]).

Since, following *Preddy*, a money transfer brought about by deception will not constitute theft, there is also no stolen property which could be the subject of an offence of handling contrary to s 22 of the Theft Act 1968.

Where a defendant obtains a cheque made out in his favour by deception, there is no offence under s 15, since the chose in action represented by the cheque was never property belonging to another, but, from the moment of its creation, belonged to the defendant. *Preddy* overrules *Duru* [1973] on this point.

(b) Obtaining a money transfer

The Theft (Amendment) Act 1996 plugged the gaps in the law revealed by *Preddy* by inserting s 15A into the Theft Act 1968. This section creates an offence of obtaining a money transfer by deception, which covers the situation where one account is debited and another credited as a result of a deception. This provision would also cover the situation where the defendant obtains a cheque made out to him by deception, since, when the cheque is honoured, there will be a money transfer.

Section 24A of the 1968 Act, as amended, created an offence of dishonestly retaining wrongful credits where transfers of money to another account are obtained by theft, deception under s 15A, or blackmail. The effect of the provision is that the recipient of such a transfer will be liable under s 24A if he does not take reasonable steps to divest himself of the wrongful credit.

(c) Obtaining a pecuniary advantage by deception

Definition
Section 16(1) of the Theft Act 1968, as amended, provided:

> A person who by any deception dishonestly obtains for himself or another any pecuniary advantage shall . . . be liable . . .

Actus reus

The deception must cause the obtaining and 'deception' and 'obtaining' have the same meaning as for s 15 above.

'Pecuniary advantage' does not include any financial benefit, but is limited to the following very specific situations:

- being allowed to borrow by way of overdraft;

- taking out a policy of insurance or annuity contract, or obtaining an improvement of the terms on which the defendant is allowed to do so;

- being given the opportunity to earn remuneration or greater remuneration;

- being given the opportunity to win money by betting.

Mens rea

The requisite *mens rea* consists of two elements:

- intention or recklessness in relation to the deception;

- dishonesty.

The *Ghosh* test as to dishonesty can be given in cases in doubt.

(d) Obtaining services by deception

Definition

Section 1(1) of the Theft Act 1978 provided:

> A person who by any deception dishonestly obtains services from another shall be guilty of an offence.

Actus reus

A 'service' is broadly defined in terms of a 'benefit' that an individual would be willing to pay for (s 1(2)).

'Deception' has the same meaning as in relation to s 15 of the Theft Act 1968 and must be operative in the same way (s 5(1)).

Mens rea

The mental element for this offence consists of an intention or recklessness in relation to the deception and dishonesty. Once again, in cases of doubt concerning dishonesty, the *Ghosh* direction should be given to the jury.

(e) Evasion of liability by deception

Definitions

Section 2(1) of the Theft Act 1978 created three offences of evasion of liability by deception. It would appear that the three offences are not mutually exclusive (*R v Holt* [1981]). The offences are committed where a person by deception:

(a) dishonestly secures the remission of the whole or part of any existing liability to make a payment, whether his own liability or another's; or

(b) with intent to make permanent default in whole or in part on any existing liability to make a payment, or with intent to let another do so, dishonestly induces the creditor or any person claiming payment on behalf of the creditor to wait for payment (whether or not the due date for payment is deferred) or to forgo payment; or

(c) dishonestly obtains any exemption from or abatement of liability to make a payment . . . shall be guilty of an offence.

Actus reus

As is common to all the deception offences, the deception must be operative, in that it must cause the securing of the remission of liability.

The 'liability' must be an existing legal liability to pay, with the exception of s 2(1)(c) which encompasses future liabilities (*R v Frith* [1990]).

It would appear that the words 'secured the remission' of the liability in s 2(1)(a) denote nothing less than the total extinguishing of the legal liability to pay. However, it can be argued, as a matter of civil law, that an existing liability can never be extinguished by a deception. This is because any agreement to extinguish liability will be rendered void, or at least, voidable by deception and, therefore, will not be totally extinguished. If this argument is correct, it is difficult to see how anyone could ever be liable in relation to s 2(1)(a).

Notwithstanding the above argument, in *R v Jackson* [1983], the Court of Appeal upheld the defendant's conviction under s 2(1)(a) for using a stolen credit card to pay for petrol and other goods.

Mens rea

The *mens rea* common to all three offences under s 2 is that the defendant should be dishonest and intend to deceive or be reckless as to whether he deceives. In addition, for the s 2(1)(b) offence, there must also be an intention to make permanent default, in other words, an intention never to pay the debt.

The Fraud Act 2006

Now the offences of deception have been abolished there is only one offence of fraud (see s 1 Fraud Act 2006). This offence can be committed in three ways under ss 2–4 and deception has been removed.

Section 2 provides:

A fraud is committed by way of false representation under s 2 where D:

(a) dishonestly makes a false representation, and

(b) intends, by making the representation:

    (i) to make a gain for himself or another, or

    (ii) to cause loss to another or to expose another to a risk of loss.

Actus reus

The offence will be committed when a defendant makes either an express or implied false representation as to either fact or law. It is not necessary for there to be an actual gain or loss.

Mens rea

The defendant must know the representation is false or know it might be false or misleading. The representation must be made dishonestly (*Ghosh* applies) and the defendant must make the representation intending to make a gain for themselves or cause a loss or a risk of loss to the victim.

Section 3 creates the offence of fraud by failing to disclose information. It provides that a person commits this offence when a person:

(a) dishonestly fails to disclose to another person information which he is under a legal duty to disclose, and

(b) intends, by failing to disclose the information:

   (i) to make a gain for himself or another, or

   (ii) to cause loss to another or to expose another to a risk of loss.

Section 4 creates the offence of fraud by abuse of position which would cover trustees, bankers, solicitors for example. It is committed where a person:

(a) occupies a position in which he is expected to safeguard, or not to act against, the financial interests of another person,

(b) dishonestly abuses that position, and

(c) intends, by means of the abuse of that position:

   (i) to make a gain for himself or another, or

   (ii) to cause loss to another or to expose another to a risk of loss.

A person may be regarded as having abused his position even though his conduct consisted of an omission rather than an act.

For these new fraud offences it is not necessary for there to be an actual gain or loss. Unlike the former offences of deception fraud is a conduct crime.

Dishonestly obtaining services
The offence of obtaining services by deception under s 1(1) of the Theft Act 1978 has also been replaced with a new offence. Section 11 of the Fraud Act 2006 creates the offence of dishonestly obtaining services. This is a result crime and no deception or false representation is required. It is limited to defendants who intend to avoid payment or payment in full.

(6) MAKING OFF WITHOUT PAYMENT

Definition
Section 3(1) of the Theft Act 1978 provided:

> . . . a person who, knowing that payment on the spot for any goods supplied or service done is required or expected from him, dishonestly makes off without having paid as required or expected and with

intent to avoid payment of the amount due shall be guilty of an offence.

Actus reus

The offence will not be committed if the payment is not legally enforceable or where the supply of goods or the doing of the service is contrary to law (s 3(3)).

It seems that, for the offence to be complete, the defendant must have 'made off' by leaving the premises where payment is due (*R v McDavitt* [1981]).

Failing to pay includes leaving an inadequate amount, counterfeit notes or foreign currency. It would also include using another's cheque or credit card or leaving a cheque that will be dishonoured. No liability under s 3 arises where the defendant induces the victim to waive the right to payment by exercising a deception (*R v Vincent* [2001]).

Mens rea

The defendant must know that payment on the spot is required and intend to permanently avoid payment and to be dishonest.

(7) HANDLING STOLEN GOODS

Definitions

Section 22 of the Theft Act 1968 provided:

> A person handles stolen goods if (otherwise than in the course of stealing) knowing or believing them to be stolen goods he dishonestly receives the goods, or dishonestly undertakes or assists in their retention, removal, disposal or realisation by or for the benefit of another.

Some of the key terms used in this section are themselves subject to further statutory definition. For example, s 34(2)(b) states that 'goods' include:

> money and every other description of property except land and includes things severed from the land by stealing.

From this definition, it would appear that choses in action, such as a bank account into which money obtained in exchange for stolen property has been paid, will constitute stolen goods (*R v Pritchley* [1973]; *AG's Reference (No 4 of 1979)* [1980]).

In addition, s 24(4) makes it clear that, in order to constitute stolen property, the goods must have been obtained as a result of theft, obtaining property by deception or blackmail.

However, goods will lose their 'stolen' status if they are restored to the person from whom they were stolen or to other lawful possession or custody (s 24(3)). Thus, in *Haughton v Smith* [1975], tins of meat ceased to be 'stolen' when police took control of the lorry transporting them.

What constitutes 'custody' seems to depend on the degree of control exercised over the goods. For example, in *AG's Reference (No 1 of 1974)* [1974], the Court of Appeal was unwilling to hold that a police officer who immobilised a car, which he suspected of containing stolen goods, by removing its rotor arm had taken custody of the property.

In a situation where goods have ceased to be 'stolen' because they have been taken into lawful custody, a defendant who handles them in the belief that they are stolen could be liable for attempting to handle stolen goods contrary to s 1(1) of the Criminal Attempts Act 1981.

It should be noted that, where stolen goods have been exchanged for other forms of property, that other property may also constitute 'stolen goods'. Section 24(2) provides that, for goods to be stolen, they must be, or have been, in the hands of the thief or handler and directly or indirectly represent the stolen goods in whole or in part.

Actus reus

Modes of handling
See also table on page 92.

- *Receiving*

  Taking possession of the stolen property. It is not necessary to show that the defendant acted 'for the benefit of another'.

- *Removal*

  Moving the stolen goods from one place to another. The transportation must be for 'the benefit of another'.

Modes of handling

Mode	Action	Benefits another	Omission
Receiving	Taking into possession or control	Not necessary	↕
Removal	Movement of goods	For another's benefit	
Realisation	Sale or exchange of goods		
Disposal	Destroying or hiding		Action required
Retention	Keeping not losing		Possible by omission
NB: Arranging to do any of the above in itself is an offence			

■ *Realisation*

Selling or exchanging the stolen goods. The realisation must be 'for the benefit of another'.

■ *Disposal*

Destroying or hiding the stolen goods. The disposal must be 'for the benefit of another'.

■ *Retention*

Keeping possession of the stolen goods. The retention must be 'for the benefit of another'. It seems that a mere omission to inform the police of the presence of stolen property will not amount to retention (*R v Brown* [1970]). However, in *R v Kanwar* [1982], a defendant who deliberately misled the police as to the presence of stolen goods in her home was held to have assisted her husband in their retention.

As well as the above five modes of handling, it is also an offence to arrange to do any of these things or to assist in the removal, realisation, disposal or retention of stolen goods by another person (s 22(1)).

For the benefit of another

All the above modes of handling, with the exception of receiving and arranging to receive, require that the defendant act 'for the benefit of another'. It follows that a defendant who knowingly sells stolen goods for his own benefit will not be liable for arranging, assisting or undertaking the realisation of stolen property. The innocent purchaser would not be 'another person' within the meaning of the sub-section (*R v Bloxham* [1983]).

Otherwise than in the course of stealing

The above words, included in the definition of the offence, are necessary to prevent many instances of theft from automatically becoming handling as well. Despite the decision of the Court of Appeal in *R v Pitham and Hehl* [1977], it would seem that the phrase 'course of stealing' clearly implies a continuous rather than an instantaneous act. However, such a continuous act concept entails obvious uncertainties about precisely when the act commences and terminates. The practical solution is to allow the jury to decide this matter on a case by case basis.

Mens rea

There are two elements to the *mens rea* of handling: dishonesty and knowledge or belief that the goods are stolen.

In relation to dishonesty, the *Ghosh* test can be applied in cases of difficulty, but should not be automatically resorted to (*R v Roberts* [1987]).

A belief that the property is stolen is a purely subjective matter and should not be equated with what the reasonable person would have believed in the same circumstances (*Atwal v Massey* [1971]).

Where there is evidence that should have made the defendant suspect that the goods were stolen, the jury are entitled to infer a belief that they were stolen (*R v Lincoln* [1980]). However, mere suspicion is not to be equated with such a belief (*R v Grainge* [1974]).

In the absence of a satisfactory explanation to the contrary, a jury is entitled to infer a belief that the property is stolen where there is evidence that the defendant came into possession of the goods soon after the theft.

You should now be confident that you would be able to tick all of the boxes on the checklist at the beginning of this chapter. To check your knowledge of Offences against property why not visit the companion website and take the Multiple Choice Question test. Check your understanding of the terms and vocabulary used in this chapter with the flashcard glossary.

6

General defences

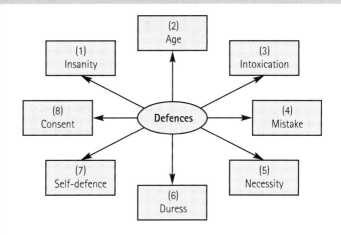

(1) INSANITY

Where the defendant claims to have been suffering at the time of the offence from some sort of mental disturbance or impairment, then automatism, insanity and, in murder cases, diminished responsibility may all be considered. Automatism, a condition which consists of the body operating without the control of the mind, and diminished responsibility have been considered above.

See table on facing page.

It should be noted that insanity, unlike automatism, will not provide a defence to crimes of strict liability (*DPP v H* [1997]).

Definition

In 1843, Daniel M'Naghten, intending to murder Sir Robert Peel, killed his secretary by mistake. Following his acquittal on grounds of insanity, the judges formulated the so called *M'Naghten* rules which have since become accepted as providing a comprehensive definition of insanity (*R v Sullivan* [1984]).

The insanity defence is available to all crimes. According to these rules, it must be proved (by the defence, on a balance of probabilities) that, at the time the offence was committed, the defendant was labouring under such a defect of reason, arising from a disease of the mind, so as not to know the nature and

Defence	Nature	When relevant	Effect of successful plea
Automatism	Body acts without control of the mind.	At the time of the offence	Not guilty
Diminished responsibility	An abnormality of mind which substantially impairs mental responsibility.	At the time of the offence	Not guilty of murder but guilty of manslaughter
Insanity	Disease of the mind which renders the defendant incapable of knowing: (a) the nature and quality of his actions; or (b) that his actions are legally wrong.	At the time of the offence	Not guilty by reason of insanity

quality of the act he was doing, or, if he did know it, that he did not know that what he was doing was wrong.

The nature and quality of the act
As we have noted, one of the two grounds for establishing insanity under the *M'Naghten* rules is that the defendant's disease of the mind prevented him from being aware of his actions. For example, in *R v Kemp* [1957], the defendant was found not guilty by reason of insanity when he was unaware of his actions during a 'blackout' caused by a disease of the body which affected the mind.

Did not know that the action was wrong
The second ground for establishing the defence is that, because of a disease of the mind, the defendant did not know that his actions were wrong. 'Wrong', in this context, has been interpreted to mean legally, as opposed to morally, wrong (*R v Windle* [1952]).

Disease of the mind
Although medical evidence will be of relevance, whether a particular condition amounts to a disease of the mind is a legal, not a medical question.

It seems that any disease which affects the functioning of the mind is a disease of the mind. Examples would include epilepsy, diabetes, arteriosclerosis and even sleepwalking (*R v Hennessy* [1989]; *R v Kemp* [1957]; *R v Burgess* [1991]).

A disease is something *internal* to the defendant, therefore: 'A malfunctioning of the mind of transitory effect caused by the application to the body of some external factor such as violence, drugs, including anaesthetics, alcohol and hypnotic influences cannot fairly be said to be due to disease' (*per* Lawton LJ in *R v Quick* [1973]).

An external cause might form the basis of a plea of non-insane automatism, provided it resulted in a total loss of control of the mind over the body.

(2) AGE

Rationale

The doctrine of *mens rea* is based on the presumption that criminal liability should only be imposed on those who are capable of understanding the nature and foreseeing the consequences of their actions. Exceptions are therefore made for children.

Children under 10 years of age

There is an *irrebuttable* presumption that a child under the age of 10 at the time of the alleged offence lacks the capacity to form the requisite *mens rea* (s 50 of the Children and Young Persons Act 1933). They are termed *doli incapax.*

Children between the ages of 10 and 14

Under s 34 of the Crime and Disorder Act 1998 children between 10 and 14 are not considered to be *doli incapax*. They are considered to be as responsible for their actions as adults. However, the defendant's young age will still be a factor in assessing the reasonableness of a defendant's actions where that is relevant (eg provocation) and also in assessing what was foreseen by the defendant in relation to crimes requiring intention or recklessness.

Children over 14 years of age

Children over 14 incur criminal liability on proof of *actus reus* and *mens rea* in the same way as adults.

Children and criminal liability

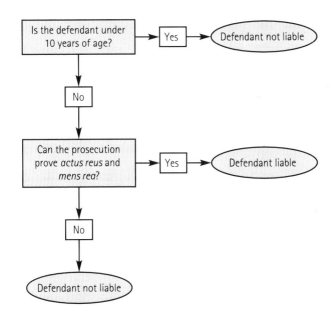

(3) INTOXICATION

The courts have distinguished between voluntary or self-induced intoxication and involuntary intoxication.

Voluntary intoxication

Self-induced intoxication is not so much a defence, but rather a denial of *mens rea* based upon mistake. Evidence of drunkenness is introduced to make the mistake more credible.

Alcohol and 'dangerous drugs'

Intoxication, negating *mens rea*, resulting from the voluntary consumption of alcohol or drugs generally recognised to be 'dangerous' will constitute a defence to crimes of *specific* intent, but not to those of basic intent (*DPP v Majewski* [1984]).

Note that s 1(2) of the Criminal Damage Act 1971 is an offence of basic intent if the prosecution allege that it was committed recklessly and one of specific intent if they allege that it was committed intentionally.

It should be noted that, where the defendant deliberately becomes intoxicated with the intention of giving himself 'Dutch courage' in order to commit an offence, the defence will not be allowed (*AG for Northern Ireland v Gallagher* [1963]).

Intoxication other than by alcohol or 'dangerous' drugs

Intoxication, negating *mens rea*, resulting from the voluntary consumption of 'non-dangerous' drugs will constitute a defence not only in relation to crimes of specific intent, but also in relation to those of basic intent, provided the defendant has not been reckless in consuming them (*R v Bailey* [1983]; *R v Hardie* [1984]).

Crimes of specific intent

- Murder

- s 18 of the Offences Against the Person Act 1861

- s 24 of the Offences Against the Person Act 1861

- s 1(2) of the Criminal Damage Act 1971 (where the defendant intends to endanger life)

- ss 1, 8, 9, 15, 16, 21, 22, 25 of the Theft Act 1968

- ss 2(1)(b), 3 of the Theft Act 1978

- s 1 of the Criminal Attempts Act 1981

- s 1 of the Criminal Law Act 1977

- Incitement

Crimes of basic intent

- Assault and battery

- ss 20, 23, 47 of the Offences Against the Person Act 1981

- Manslaughter

- Rape

- s 1(1) of the Criminal Damage Act 1971

- s 1(2) of the Criminal Damage Act 1971 (where the defendant is reckless as to whether life will be endangered)

The specific/basic intent distinction

Unfortunately, there is no clear overarching principle for distinguishing between crimes of specific and basic intent. However, it is suggested, as a pragmatic guide, that crimes which can be committed recklessly will be those of basic intent and for those requiring evidence of intent, specific intent.

Recent case law has considered whether a specific intent offence is one of 'ulterior intent', however, it appears unlikely that this will be the case where the crime is murder or a s 18 offence (see *Heard* [2007]).

Involuntary intoxication

Involuntary intoxication which negates *mens rea* will be a defence to crimes of both basic and specific intent. Involuntary intoxication which does not negate intent will not provide a defence (*R v Kingston* [1994]).

If the defendant knows that he is drinking alcohol, but is mistaken as to its strength, the rules relating to voluntary intoxication apply (*R v Allen* [1988]).

See diagram on p. 102 for summary.

(4) MISTAKE

Mistake of fact

A mistake of fact is a defence where it prevents the defendant from forming the *mens rea* for the crime in question. For example, if an individual, in a field, shoots a victim dead with a crossbow from a long distance, honestly believing he was firing at a scarecrow, the defendant would lack the necessary *mens rea* for murder, ie the intention to kill or cause grievous bodily harm (although he may be liable for other offences).

For offences where the *mens rea* is satisfied by intention only or by recklessness, it need only be shown that the defendant had an honest belief in the mistaken fact, which need not necessarily be a reasonable belief. Though obviously the more unreasonable the mistake the less likely the jury are to believe the mistake was genuine. Note that an honest belief in consent is no longer a defence to rape: a mistaken belief as to consent must now be reasonably held (s 1 Sexual Offences Act 2003).

Intoxication: general rule and exceptions

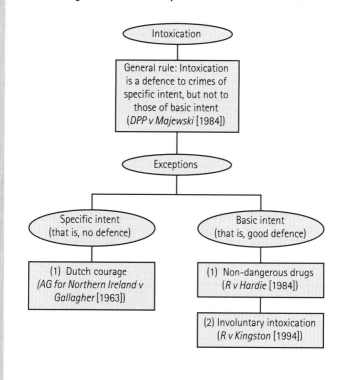

Mistake can be a defence to crimes of negligence provided that the mistake is a reasonable one, since an unreasonable mistake itself supplies the negligence on which liability is based. However, even a reasonable mistake is no defence to an offence of strict liability.

A mistake of fact made while the defendant was intoxicated should be ignored, at least in relation to the defence of self-defence. Thus, in *R v O'Grady* [1987], a defence of self-defence failed where the intoxicated defendant mistakenly believed he needed to defend himself.

(5) NECESSITY

Rationale

The essence of the defence is that the defendant committed the crime in question in order to avoid an even greater evil. There are two reasons for recognising a defence of necessity in these circumstances:

- it is unjust to punish a defendant for doing something that a reasonable person would have done in the same circumstances; and

- the law should encourage a defendant to choose the lesser and avoid the greater evil on grounds of public policy.

Availability

Despite the above rationale, the courts have traditionally been somewhat reluctant to recognise a full blown defence of necessity. Indeed, in *R v Dudley and Stephens* [1884], Lord Coleridge CJ confirmed that necessity would not be available as a defence to theft of food and then went on to doubt whether it could ever be raised as a defence to homicide.

A distinction can be made between situations where the defendant claims to be acting out of necessity by killing the victim in order to preserve his own life, and the situation where the defendant kills A in order to save the life of B, the defendant not being under any threat of harm himself. In *Re A (Children) (Conjoined twins: surgical separation)* [2000], Brooke LJ stated that in such cases the defence of necessity would be available at common law to a doctor operating to separate conjoined twins, in the knowledge that to do so would cause the death of the weaker twin, provided:

- the defendant's act is needed to avoid inevitable and irreparable evil;

- no more should be done by the defendant than is reasonably necessary for the purpose to be achieved;

- the evil inflicted by the defendant's act must not be disproportionate to the evil avoided.

THE STATUTORY DEFENCE

The following statutory provisions contain what amounts to the defence of necessity, although it is not often explicitly referred to in this way:

- s 5(2)(b) of the Criminal Damage Act 1971;

- s 1(1) of the Infant Life (Preservation) Act 1929;

- s 1(4) of the Abortion Act 1967.

Necessity at common law

During the 1980s, in cases such as *R v Willer* [1986], *R v Conway* [1989] and *R v Martin* [1989], the courts showed a greater willingness to recognise the defence of necessity, initially in relation to road traffic offences, although there has been judicial recognition that the defence is not limited to such cases (*R v Pommell* [1995]).

On the basis of *Conway* and *Martin*, it would appear that, where there is some evidence of necessity, the matter should be left to the jury with the following direction:

- had the defendant felt compelled to act by what he perceived to be the grave danger of the situation? If so,

- would a sober person of reasonable firmness sharing the characteristics of the accused have responded to the perceived threat by acting as the accused had?

If the answers to both these questions are in the affirmative, the defence of necessity, always assuming it to be available, will be established.

(6) DURESS

Duress and necessity

The defences of duress and necessity are closely related. Indeed, the courts in cases such as *Conway* and *Martin* (above) did not explicitly refer to necessity, but to 'duress of circumstances', a phrase also adopted in the Draft Criminal Code Bill of 1989. Although both defences involve a situation where the defendant is faced with a choice of two evils, the major difference between them is the source of the evil. In relation to necessity, the defendant is forced by *circumstances* to break the law, whereas in duress the source of the evil is the threat of another person.

Definition

The defence of duress consists of a plea that the defendant felt compelled to commit a crime because of an immediate threat of death or serious bodily harm by another person. For a successful defence of duress, there has to have been an imminent peril and a direct connection between the threat and the offence charged (*R v Cole* [1994]).

Availability

Because the courts want to encourage people to resist giving in to the pressures to commit crime, they have limited the availability of duress. In particular, the defence is not available in relation to murder or to an accomplice to murder (*R v Howe* [1987]) or in relation to attempted murder (*R v Gotts* [1991]). In addition, the defence is not available in relation to some forms of treason.

The defence of duress will not be available to a defendant if there is evidence that he had the opportunity to get help before the threat was due to be carried out, although regard will be had to his belief as to whether help could have been provided (*R v Hudson and Taylor* [1971]). A threat giving rise to duress can be imminent even though the threat is not one that is going to be carried out there and then (*R v Abdul-Hussain and Others* [1999]).

The defence of duress is not available to those who voluntarily join criminal groups and are then forced to commit the type of crime for which the group is renowned (*R v Sharp* [1987]).

However, if the defendant is forced to commit an offence of a type which he could not have been expected to foresee when he joined the criminal organisation, he may still be able to rely on the defence (*R v Shepherd* [1988]).

Difficulties have arisen in defining the ambit of what a defendant should be expected to foresee. For example, in *R v Harmer* [2002] the Court of Appeal held that it would be sufficient that the defendant knew that violence is used in the drugs world to enforce debts; the fact that he did not foresee that he himself would be forced to commit a violent offence was irrelevant. This would appear to contradict both *Shepherd* and *Sharp*. In *R v Z* [2003], the court recognised the conflict in the authorities. The court ruled that what has to be proved was that the accused anticipated his association with criminals could lead him, even against his will, to being involved in the type of criminality for which he is charged.

Onus of proof

If there are no facts from which the defence might reasonably be inferred in the prosecution's case, then the defendant has to produce some evidence of duress. Once this has been done, the onus of disproving duress rests on the prosecution.

The direction for duress

The direction to be given to the jury where the defendant raises the defence of duress is that laid down by the Court of Appeal in *R v Graham* [1982], as approved by the House of Lords in *R v Howe* [1987].

The jury should consider whether the defendant was compelled to act as he did because, on the basis of the circumstances as he honestly believed them to be, he thought his life was in immediate danger. If so, would a sober person of reasonable firmness sharing the defendant's characteristics have responded in the same way to the threats?

If the answers to both of these questions is 'yes', the defence of duress is established.

A characteristic of the accused of pliability or vulnerability which falls short of psychiatric illness is not a characteristic which can be attributed to the reasonable person for the purposes of the objective limb of the above test (*R v Horne* [1994]).

A mistaken belief of a defendant that he is subject to a threat of death or serious harm can form the basis for the defence of duress. This is so even when the mistaken belief is not a reasonable one (*DPP v Rogers* [1998]).

Coercion

Coercion is a special version of duress which is only available to a wife who commits an offence (other than treason or murder) in the presence of, and under the coercion of, her husband.

The defence appears to be somewhat broader than duress as it encompasses 'pressure' as well as threats of physical violence (*R v Richman* [1982]).

(7) SELF-DEFENCE AND s 3(1) OF THE CRIMINAL LAW ACT 1967

The common law allows the citizen to use reasonable force to protect his own person, his property and the person of another. In addition, s 3(1) of the Criminal Law Act 1967 permits the use of reasonable force in order to prevent crime or to arrest offenders.

Self-defence is similar to necessity and duress in the sense that the defendant will be faced with a choice of evils. The defendant will either commit a crime, perhaps homicide or a serious assault, or submit to harm being inflicted on himself, his property or the person of another.

However, unlike necessity and duress, self-defence or s 3(1) can constitute a defence to any crime, including murder and treason.

Reasonable force

Only reasonable force may be used in self-defence, defence of property or another, crime prevention and lawful arrest. However, what is reasonable depends upon the circumstances; force which might be reasonable to prevent a violent attack upon the person could be unreasonable in relation to a less serious crime.

In *Re A (Children) (Conjoined twins: surgical separation)* [2000], Robert Walker LJ suggested that if a 6-year-old child firing a gun indiscriminately in a school playground was shot and killed by a defendant to prevent further harm, the defendant would be able to rely on the defence of self-defence at common law.

In assessing the reasonableness of the force used, the jury should be directed to take into account the defendant's physical characteristics but not those relating to his mental health (*R v Martin* [2002]).

In *R v Williams (Gladstone)* [1984], it was established that the defendant commits no offence if the force used was reasonable in the circumstances *as he believed them to be*. Thus, it appears that an objective concept of reasonableness was to be applied in the context of a subjective interpretation of the circumstances (*R v Owino* [1995]).

(8) CONSENT

Commonly, consent arises as a defence in relation to assaults, although it is also a defence to theft (s 2(1)(b) Theft Act 1968). Where consent is in issue, the burden of disproving it lies on the prosecution (*R v Donovan* [1934]). In relation to assaults, two principal questions arise: (1) Did the alleged victim expressly or impliedly consent to the physical contact or force complained of? (2) If so, was that consent valid in the circumstances?

Moreover, as we have seen, with a sexual offence such as rape or sexual assault, the prosecution must prove the absence of consent and furthermore that the defendant did not reasonably believe that there was consent.

Availability

On grounds of public policy, the courts have restricted the availability of the defence. Consent is not available in relation to:

- murder or manslaughter (even if the victim begs to be killed because he is terminally ill and in intense pain);

- a fight, other than in the course of an organised sport played according to the rules (*AG's Reference (No 6 of 1980)* [1981]);

- the deliberate infliction of bodily harm for no good purpose (*R v Brown and Others* [1993]).

However, the courts are prepared to allow the defence in relation to:

- lawful sporting activities that are played according to the rules;

- medical and dental treatment carried out by qualified practitioners;

- rough horseplay, where the victim has consented to the risk of harm (*R v Jones* [1987]; *R v Atkin and Others* [1992]);

■ tattooing and, it would appear, the type of branding which occurred in *R v Wilson* [1996], where a man branded his initials on his wife's buttocks at her request.

Consent obtained by deception

Consent may be invalid where the person giving it has no real understanding of what he is consenting to (*Burrell v Harmer* [1967]). However, it is sometimes argued that, as long as the victim understands what he is consenting to, that consent is not invalidated by fraud or misunderstanding as to the circumstances. For example, in *R v Richardson* [1998] a dentist was not guilty of assaulting her patients when she failed to tell them that she had been struck off the register. However, consent was invalid in *Tabassum* [2000], where a woman consented to breast examinations on the basis that the defendant was medically qualified, which he was not: 'There was consent to the nature of the act, but not its quality.' Consent to sexual intercourse obtained by impersonation of the victim's husband or boyfriend will not be valid (*R v Elbekkay* [1995]).

You should now be confident that you would be able to tick all of the boxes on the checklist at the beginning of this chapter. To check your knowledge of General defences why not visit the companion website and take the Multiple Choice Question test. Check your understanding of the terms and vocabulary used in this chapter with the flashcard glossary.

7

Putting it into practice . . .

Now that you've mastered the basics, you will want to put it all into practice. The Routledge-Cavendish Questions and Answers series provides an ideal opportunity for you to apply your understanding and knowledge of the law and to hone your essay-writing technique.

We've included one exam-style essay question, reproduced from the Routledge-Cavendish Questions and Answers series to give you some essential exam practice. The Q&A includes an answer plan and a fully worked model answer to help you recognise what examiners might look for in your answer.

QUESTION 1

[For a practice to be subject to the criminal sanction] it is not enough in our submission that [it] is . . . regarded as immoral. Nor is it enough that it should cause harm. Both of these are minimal conditions for action by means of the criminal law, but they are not sufficient.

Clarkson, CMV and Keating, HM, *Criminal Law: Text and Materials*
London: Sweet & Maxwell, 1990, p 25

Discuss.

Answer plan

The quotation expresses the commonly held view that immorality and harmfulness are necessary but not sufficient conditions of criminal liability; that the legislator ought to consider further matters when deciding whether to criminalise or legalise particular conduct. The starting point in answering this question is the well known 'debate' of the 1950s and 1960s between Lord Devlin and Professor Hart:

the 'moral' theory: the Wolfenden Committee and Lord Devlin's response to the Report;

criticisms of the 'moral' theory – its irrationalism;

the 'harm' principle;

the limitations of the 'harm' principle;

considerations additional to the supposed immorality or harmfulness of the behaviour – the social effects of prohibition and enforcement;

is immorality a 'necessary' condition?

ANSWER

In 1959, Lord Devlin delivered the Maccabean Lecture in Jurisprudence of the British Academy under the title 'The enforcement of morals', in which he argued that the legislature is entitled to use the criminal law against behaviour which is generally condemned as immoral.

The catalyst for Lord Devlin's thesis was the *Report of the Wolfenden Committee on Homosexual Offences and Prostitution*, 1957. The Committee had recommended that homosexual behaviour between consenting adults in private should no longer be a criminal offence. The Committee thought it was not the function of the law to intervene in the private lives of citizens or to enforce any particular morality except where it is necessary to protect the citizen from what is offensive or injurious and to provide protection against exploitation and corruption.

Lord Devlin disagreed. He contended that there are no limits to the power of the State to legislate against immoral behaviour: 'immorality' is a necessary and sufficient condition of criminalisation.

He based his argument upon the premise that social harmony will be jeopardised if morality is not underwritten by the law. According to this view, tolerance of immorality threatens the social fabric, and therefore the legislature should criminalise behaviour where it is clear that there is a 'collective judgment' condemning the behaviour in question. Lord Devlin argued that morality forms a 'seamless web'. By this metaphor, he intended to convey the notion that 'society's morals' form a fragile structure and that if morality is not generally reinforced by legal means, then damage to the entire structure will follow.

According to Lord Devlin, immorality is what every 'right-minded' person considers to be immoral. If the behaviour in question provokes feelings of disgust and indignation in this 'individual', then it should be subject to the criminal sanction. Lord Devlin suggested that the judiciary are particularly well placed to express the appropriate standards by virtue of their familiarity with the 'reasonable man in the jury'.

There are a number of objections to Lord Devlin's thesis; the principal criticisms relate to its rejection of rationality. Instead of rational argument and empirical investigation of the effects of criminalisation or legalisation, Lord Devlin advocated that we place our reliance upon presumptions about the feelings of the right-minded individual and assumptions about the societal effects of liberalisation and tolerance.

Opponents of Devlin's thesis argue that although the feelings of the community are an important consideration, they cannot be the sole basis for deciding whether behaviour is to be subject to the criminal sanction, and if the revulsion of the ordinary person is a dangerous basis for criminalisation, then reliance on judicial estimates of that disgust is even more dangerous. Bentham warned us to be suspicious when officials claim that they are acting in the name of 'right-minded people'. In many cases, 'popular opinion' is used as a pretext to justify the prejudices of the legislators themselves (*Theory of Legislation*, 1876).

With reference to Lord Devlin's assertion that morality forms a seamless web, Professor Hart claimed in *Immorality and Treason* (1959) that there is no evidence that people abandon their moral views about murder, cruelty and dishonesty purely because a practice which they regard as immoral is not punished by law.

He argued that the proper approach to determining whether the criminal law should intervene involves full consideration of the social consequences of the conduct in question. To this extent, he advocated the liberal approach, which stresses the importance of rational analysis in terms of the possible harmful consequences of the conduct. The principle of democracy may require the legislator to consider the values of the 'moral majority', but the liberal tradition urges that the autonomy of the individual be respected and that individuals have rights that may trump majority preferences. Professor Hart argued that a reasoned assessment of the harmful effects of the behaviour is a far superior approach to the question of whether it should be outlawed than simple reliance on the feelings of disgust that the behaviour might cause us to feel.

The general approach of this tradition was expressed by John Stuart Mill in his essay, *On Liberty*. He maintained that the exercise of force over an individual is justified only if it is done to prevent harm to others. The fact that the behaviour might cause harm to the person who performs it is no justification for criminalisation.

Harm, however, is not to be understood as restricted to 'physical harm', but to include the violation of any recognised interest (Gross, H, *A Theory of Criminal*

Justice, Oxford: OUP, 1979). Professor Hart contended that cruelty to animals should be outlawed, although there is no harm caused to other people. In addition, legal intervention may be appropriate to restrain young people from certain activities. This is justified not on the grounds that the behaviour may cause harm to the young person, but on the grounds that such a person is not sufficiently mature to appreciate the dangers of the behaviour in question.

It might be supposed that harm theorists would be opposed to legislation controlling narcotics or compelling the use of seat belts in motor vehicles, on the basis that legislation of this type involves a violation of the fundamental principle of individual autonomy. The harm theorist is opposed to legislation designed to protect the individual from himself.

In fact, legislation of this type is often supported by modern harm theorists. They point out that the prohibited behaviour is potentially harmful to others. In 'The role of law in drug control', Kaplan explains that there are different categories of harm, any one of which may be used to justify the criminalisation of behaviour that at first sight appears only to expose the actor to the risk of harm. The individual who drives a car without wearing a seat belt or the person who consumes drugs may expose others to a 'public ward harm'. That is, he may impose on others the cost of rectifying the damage he causes himself. He may be rendered incapable of discharging economic responsibilities he owes to others ('non-support harm'). Alternatively, a case may be made out that if the individual is allowed to indulge in certain behaviour, other susceptible individuals may copy or 'model' the behaviour and suffer harm as a consequence.

This reveals one of the limitations of the liberal 'harm' theory. When secondary harms are taken into account, the theory appears to lack precision. As Kaplan points out, if we acknowledge the broad concept of harm, there are few actions that one can perform that threaten harm only to oneself.

Moreover, the prohibition of particular harmful conduct may, in itself, result in harmful consequences. For example, the sale of certain commodities (heroin, alcohol, sugar, petrol, hamburgers, etc.) may directly or indirectly cause physical harm to consumers. However, prohibiting the sale of those commodities will cause economic harm to the business enterprises involved, and so we must weigh the harms resulting from tolerance against the harms of prohibition.

In *Principles of Morals and Legislation* (1781), Bentham recognised that in this process, careful consideration should be given to the general effects of prohibition. Even though certain behaviour may be regarded as immoral or harmful, it should not be prohibited if punishment would be inefficacious as a deterrent or the harm caused by prohibition would be greater than that which would be suffered if the behaviour was left unpunished.

For example, it is sometimes argued that as the demand for certain commodities and services (for example, prostitution, abortion, alcohol and other drugs) is relatively inelastic, there is little point in criminalisation of the behaviour concerned. Indeed, it is suggested that criminalisation may make matters worse. Prior to legalisation, backstreet abortions were carried out in conditions of great risk to the mother. Legalisation permits official control, allowing matters of public health to be addressed. Similarly, if prostitution were decriminalised, one condition of operating as a licensed or registered prostitute might be periodic health checks.

In addition, the criminalisation of certain types of conduct (for example, the possession of drugs) requires, for reasons of enforcement, intrusive forms of policing, involving, for example, powers of stop and search. There is the danger that these powers might be used in a discriminatory and oppressive manner against particular groups. The outlawing of homosexual behaviour meant that the police were often involved in dubious and degrading practices to catch offenders.

Thus, the fact that behaviour is harmful to others cannot be a sufficient condition of prohibition. The virtue of the harm theory is that, at least, it focuses attention on the empirical issues concerning the social effects of the conduct and the effects of legal intervention – issues which the moral principle patently ignores.

The quotation suggests that immorality is a necessary condition of criminalisation. Is this correct? What importance should be attached to the moral feelings of a section of the community?

It is sometimes argued that support for the law is stronger where the prohibited conduct is perceived by a significant section of the population to be immoral. It is submitted, however, that immorality ought not to be regarded as even a necessary condition of prohibition. Much of modern criminal legislation (for example, road traffic laws) is concerned with conduct which would not ordinarily be termed 'immoral', but one would be hard-pressed to deny the need for that legislation.

In any case, where behaviour is perceived to be immoral, it is normally supported by empirical claims expressed in terms of the harmful consequences, real or imagined, that will result if the behaviour is tolerated. For example, Lord Devlin believed that tolerance of homosexuality would result in harm – that is, damage to society at large. If this hypothesis were testable, and if there were empirical evidence in its support, it would provide a very good argument in favour of prohibiting homosexuality.[1] On the other hand, the assertion that 'homosexuality should be prohibited because it is immoral' cannot be evaluated in the same way.

It is right that the debate should be focused on empirical claims. It is only by insisting upon arguments articulated in terms of the social consequences of tolerance, on the one hand, and prohibition, on the other, that a rational analysis of the fairness of legal intervention can be conducted.

The fact that a section of the community feels that certain behaviour is immoral cannot be either a necessary or a sufficient condition of prohibition. Although it may be prudent on some occasions for the legislator to acknowledge the 'feelings' of a section of the community – to ignore those irrational sentiments may result in the harmful consequence of social unrest – he should not rely upon the 'stomach of the man in the street'. Disgust or revulsion ought never to replace careful investigation of the social effects of prohibition.

Think point
1   Emperor Justinian believed that homosexual behaviour was the cause of earthquakes.

Each Routledge-Cavendish Q&A contains fifty essay and problem-based questions on topics commonly found on exam papers, complete with answer plans and fully worked model answers. For further examination practice, visit the Routledge-Cavendish website or your local bookstore today!